Why
People
Don't
Buy
Things

HARRY WASHBURN • KIM WALLACE

Why People Don't Buy Things

Five Proven Steps
to Connect with Your Customers
and Dramatically Increase
Your Sales

PERSEUS BOOKS
Reading, Massachusetts

The authors wish to thank their clients who kindly offered permission for their case studies to be used in this book. Please note that certain proprietary data and information have been disguised to protect client confidentiality.

Many of the designations used by manufacturers and sellers to distinguish their products are claimed as trademarks. Where those designations appear in this book and Perseus Books was aware of a trademark claim, the designations have been printed in initial capital letters.

Library of Congress Catalog Card Number: 98-88090

ISBN 0-7382-0012-3

Perseus Books is a member of the Perseus Books Group

Jacket design by Suzanne Heiser
Text design by Faith Hague
Set in 11-point Meridien by Faith Hague

123456789-DOH-0201009998
First printing, November 1998

Perseus Books are available at special discounts for bulk purchases in the U.S. by corporations, institutions, and other organizations. For more information, please contact the Special Markets Department at HarperCollins Publishers, 10 East 53rd Street, New York, NY 10022, or call 212-207-7528.

Find us on the World Wide Web at:
http://www.aw.com/gb/

*This book is dedicated to all the sales men and women
who wonder why that big one got away.*

Contents

Acknowledgments

From both of us:
Al Ries and Jack Trout for creating Positioning, which has
    changed the way people think about selling ever since;
Lee DuBois for showing us how critical it is to know where you
    are in the sale.

From Harry Washburn:
Bill Knox for showing me the great salesmen of our era;
Don Clarkson for demonstrating the power of the unexpected in
    selling;
Ted Levitt for curing my Marketing Myopia;
Tom Griffin for showing me how to make a decision;
Peter Falcone for demonstrating what leadership is;
Mal McDougall for creating the Accepted Premise;
John Pearson for showing how to make a picture worth two
    thousand words;
Terry MacDonald for unleashing the power of logic in
    advertising.

From Kim Wallace:
My grandmother, Claire Mayo, for giving me my first sales
    "gig". . .a lemonade stand;
Vince D'Onofrio for teaching me "There's No Place Like 'Om";
Clark Smidt for showing me what friendship is all about;
Mary Lewis Thorne for always being there;
Kim Wallace Sr. for demonstrating the value of a good laugh;
Dave Anderson for being the best boss ever;
Charles Laquidara for helping to open "my mind's eye."

And, again, from both of us:
Our editor Nick Philipson, our agent and guide Dick Luecke, Stu-
    art Kirsch, copy editor Theresa Cassaboom, and help and sup-
    port from Howard Gardner, Ted Jursek, Ray Comeau, Dwight
    Gertz, Justin Kaplan, Kevin Clancy, Ron Kolgraf, Tad Cantril,
    Sean Carmody, Janice DiGirolamo, and Dick Bruno.

Chapter
1

Talk the Talk.
Walk the Walk.
Tell the Tale.

You can't sing songs if you ain't got nothin' to say.

WILLIE NELSON

Why Read This Book?

Remember the last time you lost a sale to a competitor when you clearly had a better product and the right price?

Remember the last time a prime prospect said "Your client list is very impressive. I'd like to think it over and get back to you next week," but never bought anything?

Remember the last time a purchasing manager told you that "You have an excellent product line but we feel satisfied with our current supplier"?

Remember all those times you made the perfect sales presentation but sensed that for some reason your prospects had simply tuned you out?

To most of us, these experiences are worse than losing a legitimate argument, because we know they should have bought from us. Somehow, we just hadn't connected with them. Let's face it, there are times when our price is not the best or our product is clearly inappropriate. In these cases, we don't blame ourselves. But losing what should have been a sure-fire sale makes even the veteran salesperson feel puzzled, inept, and empty, wondering "Why didn't they buy? What did I do wrong?"

If these experiences are familiar, read this book.

Read it because you don't see a clear path to achieving better sales performance. Read it because your gut tells you that your current playbook is out of date. Read it because you know that the old way of thinking about selling just isn't working anymore. Read it because you're hungry for the next big selling opportunity. Above all else, read it because your future depends on a more intuitive, powerful, and intelligent selling process.

Traditional sales methods urge you to build bridges of empathy and trust between yourself and your customer by becoming a more effective listener. They tell you how to make an airtight presentation, and how to overcome objections. They encourage you to identify customer needs and match them against the features offered by your products. These approaches to selling are still valuable and worthy of study and practice. But they're getting tired. They're the *same old stuff*, and everyone uses them.

Buying Path Selling

This book is about Buying Path Selling, a system of powerful new research-proven techniques that will take your sales performance to higher levels than you've ever reached before. Buying Path Selling will help you achieve a new level of power and knowledge that will dramatically reduce your lost sales. It will help you see, feel, and hear where your prospect is at every step of the buying process. And it will show you what to say, show, and do to persuade the prospect to make a decision in your favor at every step in the buying path.

Buying Path Selling can do these things because it takes advantage of the way each individual prospect approaches the buying decision. It puts you and your customer on the same path, together. The results are not just better, they are dramatically different from what you've ever experienced.

It's Time to Change the Way We Sell

Everyone in sales—including your competitors—knows the traditional techniques and uses them every day. It's the same old stuff. Years of exposure have made customers familiar with them too. Follow those techniques and you will achieve the same level of success as everyone else—that is, you will be *average*. Work extra hard and you'll probably do somewhat better than average. But your performance will not be truly outstanding.

Few experienced salespeople, however, are satisfied with being average. That's why they are in sales. Underachievers almost never look for sales jobs—that's why God created corporate staff jobs!

We'd bet money that you aren't an underachiever and that you're not satisfied with the *average*. Why else would you be reading this book? So, if you find yourself stuck on a sales *plateau*, if the daily dose of rejection is making you numb and glum, or if you're driven simply to *win*, then you need selling tools that go beyond the same old stuff.

This sales book is very different from others you've read. This is not a compilation of *tips* for getting past gatekeepers or those nasty voice mail machines. It offers no *time-tested secrets* for closing the sale or overcoming customer resistance. There are no *hot buttons* to push. That's the old stuff. The old stuff views sales as a contest between you and the people you're trying to do business with. The new stuff doesn't tell you how to bludgeon customers into buying. Instead, it helps you understand *why people don't buy*, and shows you how to sell to them *the way they want to buy*. It doesn't view sales resistance as a barrier but as a source of information on how the customer is processing a decision.

That customer buying process is the key to Buying Path Selling.

Traditional methods view salesmanship as a process of several steps that the salesperson must go through. Buying Path Selling shifts the focus to the customer, to the critical steps that the *prospect* goes through in making a purchase decision.

A process, in management-speak, is a series of value-adding steps that create an output. Your company has a process for verifying and accounting for your out-of-pocket expenses and issuing you a reimbursement check. Its order fulfillment department has a process for handling and billing the sales you generate.

The customer faced with a buying decision likewise follows a process of several key steps. The chapters that follow will help you understand this process and will show you what you can do at each step, to facilitate the decision, and to improve the odds that it will be made in your favor.

We call our approach Buying Path Selling because it is a clear, step-by-step method for sales success based on the "buying path" of a prospect. This method is the product of over six hundred research studies and twenty years of work with companies like AT&T, Blue Cross/Blue Shield, CBS, Citibank, Gillette, Harvard University, Hilton Hotels, IBM, Macy's, Massachusetts General Hospital, and Polaroid. It works because it gives you a selling strategy for discovering and following the prospect's decision process. It replaces the combative attitude of traditional *push* selling with the persuasive *pulling* power of cooperative decision making.

Buying Path Selling explains how people *really* make purchase decisions—why they buy and why they don't. Once you understand this approach and have mastered its steps, your selling performance will improve immediately. Over time, it will continue to take you to an even higher level. Selling will become more natural, more rewarding, and more fun. You'll find that you can use these techniques to sell prospects, sell your managers, outsell your colleagues, and sell yourself in almost any situation. You will reap the rewards of superior performance.

Why the Selling Is Getting Harder: Time Is the Enemy

Most sales, marketing, and advertising people agree: selling is getting harder every day. Competition is more intense than it used to be. There are more companies from more countries selling to buyers, both corporate or consumer, who have less time and attention to pay to your message than ever before. It's harder to get in the door, whether it's the corporate door or the door to the consumer's mind. And when you do get in, prospects seem to be less interested in new ideas.

Our research shows that the great enemy of informed buying

procedures is time—the customer's time. People don't have the time they once had for considering new ideas and new products. Downsizing and job insecurity have forced people to work harder and longer, leaving them with less time to consider change. Many more women are working, and people have less time for leisurely shopping. Time famine is rampant. As the bumper sticker says: "So Many Pedestrians, So Little Time."

To save time, people have become more defensive and less open to change. And they are getting more sophisticated and quicker in deciding who to listen to and for how long. To break through these barriers, you have to know what your prospects' buying paths are, and *sell to them the way they want to buy.*

Why People Don't Buy: Miscommunication, Inattention, Wrong Argument

Traditional sales training points to *objections* as the primary reason people don't buy: people have objections to the arguments you present to them. So, in this view, your job is to *overcome* your prospects' objections by winning your arguments (i.e., by forcing the prospect to accept your point of view).

The old definition of a sales objection as a "disagreement with a particular argument" makes a number of assumptions. It assumes that your prospects are listening to you, that you are proposing arguments they care about, and that they will respond to the language and demonstrations you use to make the argument. None of these assumptions may be true.

Our research shows that most objections come in one of three types: *miscommunication, inattention,* and *wrong argument.* These are not active objections—objections over arguments of yours that your prospects actively disagree with. They are passive objections— objections that arise because you are not following the process they use to make purchase decisions. Any one of these three types of objections can derail the sale. You may not be *communicating* in a way that matches your prospects' language and personality. You may fail to gain their full *attention* because you aren't addressing the "buying step" they are struggling with. Or you may be presenting *arguments* that don't match the "buying profile" your prospects use to make buying decisions.

Avoiding the Barriers

Buying Path Selling takes you around the barriers of miscommunication, inattention, and wrong argument that lead to lost sales. It shows you how to communicate with language and demonstrations that your prospects intuitively use and respond to. It shows you how to determine which buying step your prospects are on, and how to gain their full attention at each step. It also shows you how to determine the buying profile your prospects use to make buying decisions, and which types of arguments work best in each profile. It shows you how to walk with your prospects down their personal buying paths and guide them towards making decisions in your favor at each step until the sale is concluded.

You will notice a distinct difference when you and your prospects are on the buying path together. You will communicate more effectively because you will be speaking their language. Prospects will be more interested in your arguments because you will be addressing their immediate personal decision-making concerns. You won't waste your time because you won't be wasting theirs. No more blank stares or finger drumming. No more polite refusals. No more wondering why nothing happened. And once you make the sale, it will stay sold.

Buying Path Selling works whether you are selling to a group, or to the CEO, or to consumers, or to your boss, or to an industrial, corporate, or institutional individual. It is also effective for creating marketing plans or preparing advertising campaigns.

Here's how it works.

Find the Path, Follow the Path

The key to Buying Path Selling is simple: Find the path, follow the path. Find your prospect's buying path, and follow it from where it starts, through its various steps, to the conclusion of the sale.

Every prospect has a preferred buying path for purchasing a particular type of product or service. The challenge is to find that path, determine where the prospect is on that path, and use the language, arguments, and demonstrations that precisely fit the way his buying decisions will be made.

If you find and follow your prospects' buying paths, you won't get lost, they won't get lost, and the sale won't get lost.

Talk the Talk: Language Mirroring

To communicate persuasively with prospects, you must *speak their language*. Literally. Psychologists call this "language mirroring." You must use the words and phrases, and even the body language, that your prospects use. In order to do that, you must discover as quickly as possible which of three basic personality types your prospects fit, and which profile they communicate in when dealing with your particular type of product or service. Later in this book we'll show you how you can determine prospects' personality types by listening to the words they use, by observing their eye movements, and by noting their body type, clothing, and even their office environment.

Once you've determined a prospect's personality type, you can use the right language and demonstrations to build her trust and confidence—to convince her that you are on the same wavelength. You are then ready to determine what buying step the prospect is on, and what arguments in favor of purchasing your product or service will be most persuasive.

Walk the Walk: The DREAM Buying Path

Although it often seems like prospects make sudden single decisions to buy, they actually have to make five *decisions* in your favor before they will buy what you are selling. You have to figure out where prospects are in this series of decisions—or "steps". Once you've done that, you can use arguments that will persuade them to make that particular decision in your favor. In this book we explain the five buying steps, we make it easy for you to recognize each one, and we show you which arguments will be most persuasive at each step.

We call the five decision steps the "DREAM buying path." This makes it easy to remember and focus on when you're in the midst of a sales call. Here are the five steps:

D DO step
R REPEAT step
E EVALUATE step
A ACCESS step
M MONEY step

Here's what happens at each step:

1. **DO** *something or nothing.* Prospects must decide that they need to DO something. For example, the corporation's office PCs are so old and over-the-hill that they *should be* replaced. But if the prospect hasn't already decided to DO something about your category of product or service, this buying step must be addressed first with arguments that will motivate action. Bypassing this step by attempting, for instance, to show why your product is better than the competition when the prospect is not yet motivated to take action, will likely lose the sale for you.

2. **REPEAT** *or* **NOT REPEAT**. If prospects are ready to DO something, and they have bought the product or something similar before, they must decide whether or not to REPEAT how they bought the last time. For instance, the office manager must decide whether to simply upgrade her PCs by buying the same vendor's newest model, or whether to seriously investigate alternatives. With customers who have bought from you before, you should obviously uncover and reinforce the most positive aspects of that experience. But with prospects who have not bought from you before, you must convince them to NOT REPEAT buying from a previous vendor or source. In this case, you must attack this buying step by breaking their pattern of loyalty or habit. You must create serious doubt in their minds about the wisdom of their behavior.

3. **EVALUATE** *a new choice.* When prospects are ready to DO something, and convinced to NOT REPEAT a cycle with a competitor, they are ready to EVALUATE new choices. Here is your golden opportunity to make use of your prospects' intuitive buying profiles to present the arguments that will be most powerful for them, and to deliver those arguments with the language and demonstrations that are most persuasive for them. This is where you can *Tell the Tale* in the most powerful way.

4. **ACCESS:** *Where to Buy It?* Once the decision to buy has been made, prospects must decide where to ACCESS or

purchase the product or service. You must make sure they buy from you. The last thing you want to do is convince someone to buy and then have them buy the product from someone else. This is particularly important when products and services with similar features are widely available from many sources. The PC salesperson, for example, may find that he has successfully persuaded the office manager that her sixty desktop units must be replaced, only to lose the sale to a vendor offering equivalent computing power with slightly different features.

5. *MONEY: What price?* In the final buying step, prospects must agree that your price is within an acceptable range.

As you probably suspect, the five steps on the buying path might take only a few minutes to complete, or they might take months or even years. In any case, if they buy from you, they must make a decision in your favor at each step.

Each buying step has its own dynamics. These dynamics are covered in detail in chapters 3 through 13. Together, they give you everything you need to know and use to be successful at each step.

Tell the Tale: The Three Buying Profiles

All prospects intuitively prefer to use one of three buying profiles when making purchase decisions, particularly when Evaluating New Choices. Buying profiles are a reflection of how prospects represent and deal with the world around them. Buying profiles are part of prospects' personality types, and are the essence of their personal buying strategy. Most importantly, when you know what buying profile your prospects are using to make purchase decisions, you have a very strong indicator of what specific types of sales arguments will be most persuasive to them. In our terminology, a prospect, may be a Thinker, a Commander, or a Visualizer. While the details of these profiles and the arguments they find most compelling are spelled out in chapters 8, 9, and 10, we can say here that:

➡ The gut-feel, take-charge *Commander* is people and action oriented, and concerned with leadership and reputation.

- The *Thinker* is an analytical type, inclined to use logic, rules, and linear thinking procedures to make decisions.
- The *Visualizer* likes speed and immediate results, and responds to visual, tangible features and cosmetic appearance.

The buying profile is a key element of Buying Path Selling. Once you understand the buying profile of a particular prospect, you'll be in a position to use *specific* sales arguments, language, and demonstrations tailored to Tell the Tale with great persuasive power.

Tangible Results Now

That's Buying Path Selling in a nutshell. Details and examples from the trenches of sales, marketing, and advertising are provided—including the five big mistakes and thirty-one lost opportunities—in the chapters that follow.

Once you understand the five buying steps and three buying profiles, you will see each new sales situation with new eyes. Whenever you find prospects who are at a different buying step than the one you expected, or whenever you discover that prospects fit a different buying profile than your own, you will know how to switch quickly to the *prospect's* step and profile. You will see immediate tangible results: prospects will become more attentive, more responsive to your arguments, and more comfortable with you. You'll have avoided the barriers of miscommunication, inattention, and wrong argument. You and your prospects will be *on the same wavelength*, and you will dramatically increase your chances of sales success. You'll feel better about your work, knowing that you are giving prospects and customers the best possible opportunity to evaluate what you offer on their own terms, without wasting their time or yours, and without trying to sell them in a way they don't want to buy.

Chapter

2

Rita Buys Her Dream Car

Gentlemen prefer blondes.

Anita Loos

THIS STORY ACTUALLY happened to me (Harry Washburn) a few years ago. It was a wonderful chance to watch, and hopefully help, a determined friend cope with a difficult and important purchase decision. The outcome was totally unexpected, but seems perfectly reasonable after the fact.

The phone rang suddenly, disturbing my usual quiet Sunday afternoon of reading the *New York Times* and *Boston Globe* while sunning myself on the back deck.

It was Rita. "Harry, I don't know what to do. I can't figure it out. When I put my car in first gear nothing happens. I'm stuck here at the stoplight on Garden Street and Linnean. It won't move, but the engine's running okay, I think. What should I do? Can you drive over and help me?"

Rita was an old friend. She was intelligent and resourceful, an analytical type who enjoyed thinking about things and figuring them out. She had a talent for computers and was doing very well with the arcane twists and turns of a tough course on computer assembly language programming. Like some analytical types, she was an accomplished musician, playing both classical and popular piano. Unlike the techie stereotype, she was concerned about her visual appearance, she was a snappy dresser—who actually designed and sewed some of her own clothes—and she dyed her hair blonde. She had little interest or experience in physical or mechanical things, and this car situation had her baffled.

Her car was a faithful thirteen-year-old Dodge that had served her well beyond its years. I had watched it age to the point where repairs were becoming more frequent, more expensive, and more aggravating. It was clearly at the end of its life span. I had suggested several times in the past year or so that Rita sell it, but she refused, thinking it had a few more miles left in it. My sense was that the miles had run out this time.

"Forget first gear," I said. "Try putting it in second to get it moving. Use plenty of gas pedal and let the clutch out slowly. If that doesn't work, call me and I'll come over. Or call me from home if you get there."

Rita could be stubborn. She called me from home and said, "Second gear works just fine. How much will it cost to fix first gear?"

"About three or four times what the car is worth," I guessed.

As I expected, she wouldn't take my word for it. She called Rick, her favorite car mechanic whom she trusted implicitly—I admit he does excellent work at a fair price. He confirmed that it would be silly to spend $200 or so to repair the transmission. The Dodge was history. Trade-in value was maybe $50. Tops. So Rita decided to buy a new car. New for her, anyway.

Rita had originally bought the Dodge used for $2,200 with about five years and 55,000 miles on it. It lasted another eight years and 61,000 miles. $275 and 7625 miles a year. Not bad. Pretty good, in fact. So good that she decided to find another car just like it, or at least another one that would give her the same return on an investment under $3,000. She also wanted the same features that were important to her; four doors for easy use of a roomy back seat, plenty of trunk space, and no unnecessary frills like automatic transmission, power steering, air conditioning, or a stereo cassette radio. Just basic, economical transportation.

Rita started by looking through the *Boston Sunday Globe* for used cars. Not much help. On the one hand, she didn't want to buy a car from an individual because she would have no recourse if a mechanical problem turned up. That eliminated the FSBO listings. On the other hand, the dealer ads rarely showed a used car more than three years old, and most were loaded and priced above $8,000, so there was not much help there either. Time to hit the pavement.

The Automile, off route 128 outside Boston, is a conglomeration of fifty or so car dealers stretching three miles along Route 1. It includes megadealers like Ernie Boch, the largest car dealer in New England, and bargain used car dealers selling "Mechanics Specials" that need the frame bent back or something worse. It's the place to go when you don't know where else to start.

After three days of scouring the Automile, it became clear to me that used cars under $3,000, with even just a few of the characteristics Rita wanted, didn't exist. Anything in her chosen price range was a mechanic's nightmare, a used car from hell, or close to it. Anything that fit a fair number of her other specifications was way too expensive. Rita was in a funk for a week. What now? The clutch in the old car was starting to get raggedy from starting in second gear. Something had to happen.

The next Sunday the phone rang again. It was Rita. "I want to get a new red convertible with a white top," she announced. I was stunned.

"Really", I said. "How come?"

"I always wanted to be a blonde driving a red convertible with the white top down, and if I can't find the used car I want, I'm going to go all the way and get what I've always dreamed of." With Rita's hair already dyed blonde, the car was apparently the only missing piece of her dream. I figured it should be easy from here on in. No such luck.

Rita didn't want a foreign car, but most of the available convertibles were foreign makes. "What if I'm in Arkansas and it breaks down," she complained, "who'll be able to fix it?" For her, the idea of ending up in Arkansas in a sick car was like being stranded on a strange planet. I tried to convince her that getting a major brand foreign car repaired almost anywhere in the United States hadn't been a problem for decades, but she was not convinced. Besides, she said, she wanted to "buy American," which I suspect was the real reason.

At the time, the least expensive American convertible models available were the Dodge 600 and the Chrysler LeBaron. The Mustangs and Camaros were financially out of the question. Even the 600s and the LeBarons were priced around $17,000—still dramatically out of Rita's price range. Not to worry. After leafing through the *Boston Globe* again, Rita quickly realized that there was not much point in buying the Dodge 600 convertible, as it only saved about $1,000 over the Chrysler LeBaron version of the same car. The Dodge didn't look glamorous enough for her, or for me either, for that matter. And if she was going to go for broke to achieve the glamour image of her dreams, what was another thousand dollars, anyway?

So we were off to the robber baron dealers, some of them the same dealers we had visited for used cars. I noticed that at one Chrysler dealership she looked for Fred, a salesman who had impressed her in some way. When she was looking for a used car, Fred had asked her, "If you could have any car you wanted, how would you see yourself driving down the road?" She replied something to the effect that she had always wanted a convertible, but there obviously weren't any affordable used ones available. But she remembered Fred.

So Fred's was the first Chrysler dealership we approached. And Fred was glad to oblige our request for a test drive in the gleaming red LeBaron convertible that was sitting on the lot. Driving a LeBaron was an exhilarating experience. With a red paint job and the white top down, it looked sensational. Everything Rita had hoped for. She did indeed look glamorous with her blonde hair waving in the breeze. She loved the way it looked and the way she looked in it.

But New England has about sixteen weeks of good convertible weather, the rest are rain, fog, sleet, snow, the occasional nor' easter, or just plain cold. So we took another look, this time with the top up. This put Rita in a more practical frame of mind, which made the choice much more difficult. The features that Rita wanted were not available. For instance, because it was a convertible, the LeBaron was only available in a two-door model, with a smaller than normal back seat, since the foldaway top took up lots of space. And with the top up, it was nearly impossible to get anything inanimate into or out of the back seat. The trunk space was also diminished by top-raising gear, so the luggage space was minimal. Maybe enough for a one-nighter. Plus a LeBaron only came with an automatic transmission and power steering, whether you wanted it or not. You could get the LeBaron without air conditioning, but you'd have to wait eight weeks because it would be a special order, and then the resale value would suck. And so forth and so on. So much for Rita's list.

To supercharge the dilemma, the only way Rita could get the flashy wheel covers she wanted was to get Option B, which included power windows, power door locks, cruise control, and a bunch of other power things that were decidedly not on her list. Now the price tag was in the $19,000 range. Rita began to stew. Nothing much happened for a few days. But by Friday her cognitive dissonance had resolved itself and it was the red convertible with the white top and Option B or bust. Back to the dealers for the best possible price.

Several days later we were down to three dealers. Fred and the two with the lowest prices. Several salesmen had mentioned that their dealerships had outstanding service departments, but there was no way Rita was going to travel to the suburbs for service. I had never seen Rita in this kind of tough negotiator mood before. She was pushing and shoving, playing one dealer off the other. When it came down to it, all three dealers came up with prices that were pretty close. I asked one of them if he would throw in the stereo CD radio upgrade at no extra charge, and he said he would. Rita balked at the offer because she really didn't want the CD radio anyway. I noticed that even in the midst of the price negotiations, Fred would mention from time to time how great the LeBaron looked, and how great she would look in the LeBaron on the road, in town, and wherever. Meanwhile, the other dealers didn't come up with anything new so finally the deal was done. With Fred. Who else?

So that's how Rita got her dream car. It's a good thing she never found the $3,000, five-year-old, four-door sedan she was looking for, because the red LeBaron convertible with the white top made her happier than anything else she had purchased while I knew her. A dream come true.

Questions, Questions

Rita's story begs for questions to be answered. Here are just some of them:

- ● What buying path did Rita follow in buying the LeBaron?
- ● Why did she decide to buy another car in the first place? Why did she wait until then?
- ● How did she initially try to solve the problem? What opportunity did all those salesmen, except Fred, miss at this stage?
- ● What was Rita's primary buying profile when she decided to look for a new car?
- ● What other buying profiles did she slip into during the evaluation process?
- ● How did the salesmen respond to her in the new car buying process? Who did a better job? Why? How?
- ● When she made her final purchase, what did she really buy, the car, the dealership, the salesman, or what? Why?

These questions are key to understanding why people buy things, and why they don't. The rest of this book will show how people really make buying decisions, and how you can dramatically improve your sales effectiveness by selling to people the way they really want to buy.

Rita's New Car—And What Really Happens

Most salespeople feel compelled to tell the world how great their stuff is from their own point of view. The plain truth is, most prospects are not out there waiting to find out how great your stuff is from your own personal point of view. Typically they will resist finding out how great your stuff is, unless you are selling to them the way they want to buy.

As any experienced salesman knows, if an individual or group prospect has substantial objections to buying from you that are not smoked out and resolved in your favor, you will lose the sale. That's why so much sales training time is spent on *handling objections*, which really means overcoming objections. Why people don't buy things is as important a factor in individual and group purchasing decisions as why they do buy things. Many times why they don't buy is even more important than why they do buy.

Rita's story is a true one, and no doubt you have gone through similar experiences. Rita's purchase of a new car shows a person going through five major buying steps, using her own personal buying profiles. In this sense the process can look complicated if you don't know what's going on. But it's not really complicated at all. In each chapter of this book, we'll show you what goes on in each step. These will be illustrated by many business-to-business, industrial, and consumer examples of how various types of buyers handle these buying steps. But first, let's look at the three basic types of personalities that a salesperson deals with when facing a prospect.

Chapter
3

Talk the Talk: Language Mirroring Creates Trust and Confidence

Different strokes for different folks.

Folk saying

OVER THE YEARS, we've found that one of the best ways to communicate sales training points, and make them memorable so you can use them, is to illustrate them through our own experiences. That's the way the great trainers have done it, and that's what we've done throughout this book. Pardon us if it sometimes seems like an extended commercial, but people tell us that the selling techniques come alive and are much easier to remember and use this way.

Recently we were visiting John D. O'Brien, Executive Director of the Cape Cod Economic Development Council, to talk about a series of market research studies for a proposed Cape Cod Convention and Performing Arts Center. We arrived early, and were ushered into his office to wait for him. The first thing we noticed was a large display of photographs of John with a variety of famous individuals and groups of dignitaries. We saw him posed with former Massachusetts Governor Mike Dukakis, with Senator Ted Kennedy, and an especially important photo of him shaking hands with President Clinton. Other objects included several golf trophies, awards from assorted civic groups, and an old photograph of John in uniform with his college football team.

John arrived, shook hands vigorously with us, and sat down comfortably. At roughly 230 pounds he looked in good shape for his age, if not quite ready to play tackle again at Brown University. His gray suit, white shirt, and moderate tie were unexciting but politically correct. He had already taken his jacket off and rolled up his sleeves.

"I feel we have a powerful opportunity to give Cape Cod a center that will attract people here throughout the year. How can you help our team put together a winning game plan to fund this center?" John asked. "But, before you answer that, let me give you some background." With that, his eyes looked down and to his right, though there wasn't anything particular on his desktop to look at.

We knew what to do. Before we did anything else, we had to build John's trust and confidence in us, and achieve a level of rapport that would allow us to communicate our sales points with maximum impact. Because once you have established rapport with your prospects, everything else you need to accomplish to make the sale becomes easier and quicker. Once they sense that you are *on their wavelength*, they become more attentive, more relaxed, and more conversational. They understand you better, and they are more likely to believe you. Your sales will immediately increase, and as an added bonus, you'll enjoy talking with prospects more than ever before.

Three Buying Profiles: Three Languages

To build rapport and gain prospects' trust and confidence, you need to "speak their language." And to speak their language, you need to know what mode or profile they use to view the world. In the mid-1970s at the University of California at Santa Cruz, researchers Richard Bandler and John Grinder discovered through an analysis of the practices of highly successful psychotherapists that people internally "represent" the world about them in one of three different profiles. The most successful therapists were instinctively communicating with their patients in the *same profile* their patients were using. Although these successful therapists had personal communicating styles of their own, they willingly abandoned these in favor of their patients' styles. They intuitively used the same verbal and body language used by the patient. This built rapport and increased the patient's trust and confidence in the therapist. As a result, the therapist was much more likely to produce positive changes in the patient's behavior.

Bandler and Grinder called their system Neuro-Linguistic Programming, or NLP, and it has become an important part of therapist training over the years. One of the most engaging books they've written about NLP (it's actually a transcript of NLP training workshops they conducted) is *Frogs Into Princes*, published in 1979.[1] NLP has since grown into a highly successful sales training technique, with an emphasis on specific ways to establish rapport and build trust and confidence with prospects in a variety of selling situations.

In this chapter we take the NLP approach further, by showing you how to very quickly and accurately identify prospects by one of three easily remembered buying profiles: the Commander profile, the Thinker profile, and the Visualizer profile. We'll show you how to immediately identify these profiles by verbal language and eye movements, with further clues from your prospects' body language and physical body type, the clothes they wear and how they wear them—even their office environments. Then we show you how to mirror their verbal and body language to rapidly establish rapport and build their trust and confidence in you. In following chapters we show you a completely new and very powerful way to use buying profiles. We will show you which categories of sales points will be *more persuasive* for each buying profile!

The Commander Buying Profile: Taking Charge of the Action

John O'Brien was in the Commander buying profile the day we saw him, and it was clear from his surroundings that this was his usual profile. To make the Commander profile easier to understand and remember, think of General MacArthur, the Commander of the Allies in the Pacific in World War II, and one of only five, five-star Generals in the history of the United States. The dramatic picture below shows MacArthur wading ashore at Leyte on October 20, 1944 as his first step in recapturing the Philippines from the Japanese.

Corbis

Commanders are take-charge, action-oriented types who like to be leaders. Commanders are typically aggressive and competitive, with a "can-do" attitude. They like winning. It was obvious that John O'Brien wanted to win the funding game for his center.

Commanders like people, and people like them. They are team builders and like forming, working with, and leading groups of people. They are sensitive to the feelings of others. They are networkers and tend to be politically oriented, with interests in elective, appointive, and office politics. Many CEOs are Commander types. O'Brien's display of photos of himself posed with famous and not-so-famous politicians was a clue, as was his emphasis on leading his team to victory.

Commanders like to talk about feeling, action, strength, weight, dominance, and winning. O'Brien's opening sentence, "I FEEL we have a POWERFUL opportunity. . ." is just one example.

Commanders are often athletically oriented. Following are some typical examples of athletes using Commander language.

Bill Parcells, the famous football coach who has been to the Super Bowl several times, provides a classic example of Commander-speak. At a New England Patriot's press conference he once exclaimed, "I am just telling you in my HEART this is what I FEEL." And on September 8, 1998 when Mark McGwire became the new King of Clout, breaking Roger Maris's record with 62 homers, McGwire exclaimed, "This last week and a half my HEART has been RACING a million miles an hour. Earlier in the day I TOUCHED Roger Maris's Hall of Fame bat. I TOUCHED it to my HEART. It was an unbelievable FEELING."

If you watched the 1998 Winter Olympics broadcast from Nagano, Japan on CBS you heard gold medal speed skater Giana Roma tell viewers that "I skate on my FEELINGS!" And remember when Kazuyoski Fumaki looked back on winning double gold medals for his ski jumping? "I just want to find some way to keep these memories in my HEART forever!" Different countries, different languages, same Commander-speak.

Underneath, Commanders are *gut-feel* types. They are more sensitive to feelings and the sense of touch than they are to visual input or analytical thinking.

Identifying and Mirroring the Commander Profile

The words people use are powerful indicators of the buying profile they are in. If you listen carefully to the words your prospect uses, you'll be able to identify immediately which profile your prospect is in *right now.*

For instance, in his opening statement John O'Brien used five key words that Commanders like to use: "I FEEL we have a POWERful opportunity to give Cape Cod a center that will attract PEOPLE here throughout the year. How can you help our TEAM put together a WINning game plan to fund this center?" These words clearly indicated that John was in the Commander profile.

Here are key words that Commanders like to use:

feel	win
sense	team
grasp	power
touch	people
hit	friend(ly)
grab	comfortable
handle	heavy
tackle	pressure

With practice, you will be able to listen for these words and phrases even as you take note of the subject matter they are conveying. When you respond, you will be able to discuss the subject matter using the same words and phrases. This is called "mirroring." Mirroring your prospects' verbal language is one of the most powerful ways to create rapport, and to build trust and confidence.

Phrases like those offered below will put Commanders at ease and help convince them that you understand how they feel about the products or services you are discussing, and how they feel about the world in general. They will feel that you can be trusted, and will gain confidence in your ability to help them. More important, they will feel more comfortable giving you vital information about their situation, their company, and themselves. This information can prove invaluable in showing you what they need to make a decision in your favor. Try phrases like these:

We feel that. . .
I sense that you don't feel comfortable with. . .
Our development (support, etc.) team. . .
Our CEO. . .
In competitive tests. . .
Your competitors are. . .
Your team will like. . .
We can handle (tackle) the toughest assignments. . .

While the words people use are often the strongest indicator of their buying profile, there are other clues. Another key indicator is how prospects move their eyes as they talk to you. When people search their memory to access information during a conversation, they tend to divert their gaze from your face to somewhere else. Commanders tend to look *down and to their right* towards their right leg when they are accessing their memories, just as John O'Brien did in our interview with him. Perhaps the best way to remember this is that Commanders are looking for the power, and the power in an athlete (such as a boxer or a right-handed baseball batter) comes up from a firmly planted right leg.

Words used and eye movements are key indicators of prospects' buying profiles *right now*. We emphasize *right now*, because people may use more than one buying profile over the space of a sales appointment. They may switch profiles to make decisions about a particular subject area, and they may even switch profiles in the middle of an interview. If you stay aware of their words and eye movements, you'll be able to stay on top of the profile they are using, and mirror that profile with persuasive language, sales points, and demonstrations.

Almost everyone has a dominant profile that they use most often. In computerese, it is their "default" profile. When you first meet someone, or even earlier, make an effort to determine that person's dominant profile. Start your conversation in that profile, and continue in that profile until you notice that the prospect has switched to a different one. Clues to a prospect's dominant profile include body type and movement, clothes, and office environment.

Commanders will typically give you a strong, firm handshake, as John O'Brien did, and may even pat you on the back when they meet you. They like to touch you and prefer a good, strong handshake in return. Their body type is often athletic or post-athletic. If they are older, they may be on the heavy side. They like to sit comfortably and are inclined to lean back in their chairs. Their movements are strong but graceful, and not rushed. Their clothes are usually professionally appropriate, and may be expensive, but with somewhat unexciting color choices. They will wear casual clothes if they feel they can get away with it. Don't be surprised if they roll up their sleeves and loosen their ties.

Commanders' office environments express their interest in people, groups, teams, and athletics. As in John O'Brien's office, pictures of themselves with important people, receiving awards, and similar situations are strong clues. Athletic trophies and memorabilia are a dead giveaway.

Armed with the strong feeling that your prospect is a Commander, you'll be ready to get on his team and tackle the situation at hand with a winning combination of your products and services!

The Thinker Profile: Sounds Like the Logical Choice

A few years ago we received a request-for-proposal from McLean Hospital—one of the most respected psychiatric institutions in America—to meet and discuss a marketing research project for testing new service areas in the business sector. The detailed letter from the General Director of the hospital, Dr. Francis de Marneffe, outlined fourteen goals of a study along with a suggested methodology and time frame.

Our presentation group drove to Belmont, Massachusetts to meet with his group. We waited nervously in the lobby to be interviewed by Dr. de Marneffe and his staff of ten other psychiatrists. His diplomas from the University of London and Westminster Hospital were framed on the wall. Needless to say we felt slightly awkward at the notion of being *analyzed* by such a highly credentialed, analytical group. What would it take to impress them? Would war stories about our successes in health care or business make a good impression? Would they dissect our every word? If we said the wrong thing would we be ushered out the door by little men in white coats? What should we do?

The oak door to the conference room opened slowly. We were escorted into a somewhat antiquated conference room by one of the female doctors who looked like central casting's typical school librarian: thin, drab dress, glasses, and gray hair up in a bun. The psychiatrists were seated around the conference room with Dr. de Marneffe at the center. No fashion awards were going to be won by this group. They were definitely into functional attire, not high style.

Dr. de Marneffe rose to greet us. He shook hands lightly and introduced his colleagues around the table. Then he asked us to be seated at the head of the conference table so they could ask us some questions. He was a trim man with short gray hair and bushy eyebrows. He wore relatively plain looking eyeglasses, a button-down white shirt, and a conservative tan Brooks Brothers suit topped with a bow tie. We realized quickly that he was a Thinker type, as we had suspected from his letter. His words confirmed our initial impressions.

"We think the logical approach is to find new markets for services, and it sounds like the business community will prove to be the best target." He then turned to us with a list of prepared questions.

As we answered each question it appeared that Dr. de Marneffe was more interested in *listening* to our responses than in watching our delivery. He had detailed questions about the procedures of conducting business-to-business interviewing. He became somewhat more interested in our accumulated academic credentials (Dartmouth College, Harvard Business School, faculty positions at Boston University and Harvard Extension Program, and so on). A mention that one of the group's relatives had been in charge of the ENT Department at Massachusetts Eye and Ear Infirmary generated some interest, but when we started enumerating our relevant client experience, Dr. de Marneffe's eyes seemed to wander off to the right, then to the left. He wasn't impressed. We mentioned several business-to-business case studies of research we had conducted for Fortune 500 companies, but there was still little response.

The interview was going nowhere fast. We weren't really connecting on the same wavelength and we had only twelve minutes left to find the frequency of our audience and lock in. Unless we got on track immediately, we would be out of the competition. So we decided to throw caution to the wind and try something seemingly unrelated to the issue at hand.

Our research director, Jennifer Dilbeck, mentioned our work helping public television stations like WGBH in Boston. Dr. de Marneffe's ears perked up. He sat up straighter and asked, "I'd like to hear how your research assisted WGBH in their efforts. My wife enjoys their musical presentations. I personally enjoy 'NOVA' and 'Masterpiece Theater'." Something was happening.

Jennifer asked if anyone had seen the "Think Again," TV testimonial spots on WGBH Boston. They had. These spots depicted actual viewers of public TV, people who professed to love the programming, but who hadn't gotten around to contributing. The doctors were perking up. We explained how our research had been instrumental in generating a successful on-air fund-raising strategy that increased the station's unsolicited "white mail" contributions by 90 percent. We descibed the campaign to shock viewers with the fact that only a small minority of them support the station, and included the pitch "if you THINK your pledge is unimportant, THINK again. Fewer than two out of ten viewers support their favorite show. So rush your check in today."

There was a twinkle in Dr. de Marneffe's eyes and a hint of a smile on his face as he observed, "What a constructive use of guilt!" Others around the table were nodding their heads in agreement. They were now listening carefully. We had connected on their Thinker wavelength, and we were back on track. In fact, the interview ran over by fifteen minutes. When we received written notice several weeks later that we had been chosen for the study because we were considered *the logical choice*, we were delighted, but not terribly surprised.

Dr. de Marneffe was in the Thinker profile that day. His surroundings and speech made him easy to categorize. To make the Thinker profile easier to understand and remember, think of Albert Einstein. Einstein was a classic Thinker. He was one of the greatest physicists and physical mathematicians in history, and he totally changed our understanding of the physical universe and the cosmos. From his proven theories of relativity, we now know that nothing can go faster than the speed of light, and that light rays are bent by the force of gravity. His famous equation $E=mc^2$ showed that matter can be converted into pure energy, giving us the basis for nuclear energy and power. On the personal side, he was an avid amateur violinist who used to play in his kitchen because the acoustics were better there.

Thinkers like thinking because it's easy and fun for them. They want to understand how things work from a logical perspective.

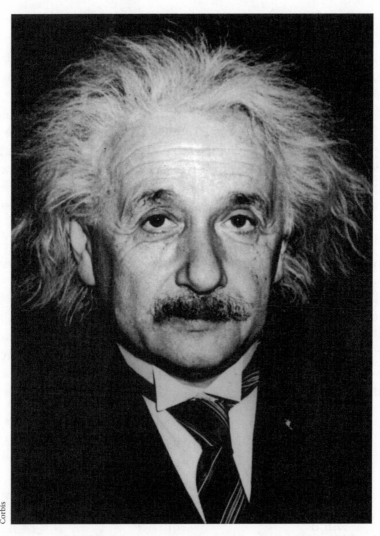

They like to analyze the details. They want to understand the underlying reasons for why things happen. They like knowing the answers, and they like advising people better than taking action directly. They like being right and they like being the expert.

Thinkers like reading, writing, listening, and education. Don't be embarrassed if they start to lecture you, they are enjoying it and will appreciate it if you listen carefully. On the other hand they can ask penetrating questions. Be straightforward. Give details. If you don't know the answer, say so, and get back to them with a detailed answer. They will appreciate the follow-up.

Thinkers are time sequence oriented and are concerned about the steps needed to accomplish something in the future. They want to know their options and the likely outcome of each. They may get stalled by "analysis paralysis," so you may need to help them move ahead more quickly.

Many Thinkers have an intellectual bent. They are often musically inclined, and many have some instrumental musical talent. They are less likely than average to be athletic. They may not be outgoing to non-Thinkers, and some are true loners. But they will respond to you if you speak their language and follow their thought processes. CFOs, engineers, scientists, and technical types are often Thinkers.

Underneath, Thinkers are analytical types. They are more sensitive to logic and the sense of hearing than they are to gut feelings or visual input.

Identifying and Mirroring the Thinker Profile

Thinkers may use a large vocabulary, but generally they use certain types of words more often. You can identify immediately if your prospects are in the Thinker profile *right now* if they are using words like these:

think	how (?)
hear	why (?)
tell	logic
talk	future
say	steps
sounds	sequence
makes sense	understand
numbers	prove
reason	know

For instance, Dr. de Marneffe used six key words that Thinkers like to use, in his opening statement: "The NUMBERS show that the FUTURE of McLeans and health care providers in general is in question. We THINK the LOGICal approach is to find new markets for services, and it SOUNDS like the business community will PROVE to be the best target."

Mirroring a Thinker's profile by using phrases like those listed below will put Thinkers at ease and help convince them that you understand how they think about the products or services you are discussing, and how they think about the world in general. They will start to trust you, and will gain confidence that you can help them. To help obtain a decision in your favor, try phrases like these:

> I think that. . .
> It sounds like you need. . .
> I hear what you're saying about. . .
> I understand the problem you have. . .
> Here are the reasons behind. . .
> Our Chief Scientist. . .
> Here are the numbers:. . .
> There are several steps to the solution. First. . .

When Thinkers search their memories to access information, they usually look *straight to the left side or the right side,* just as Dr. de Marneffe did in our interview with him. An easy way to remember this is that Thinkers consider themselves levelheaded logical types, so they'll look for memory on a level horizon. (They may occasionally look down and to their left when trying to figure out the implications of what you said, but they are not accessing memory.)

Thinkers may or may not give you a handshake, so don't be put off if they don't, and don't force a handshake—they won't like it. They may react negatively to touching, such as a pat on the back. This can indicate to them that you are definitely not a thinker, which can make communication and the building of trust and confidence more difficult, perhaps impossible. If you have had a pleasant, productive interview, a parting handshake is common.

Thinker body types tend towards thinner and less athletic profiles. They may appear to be slightly more nervous than average. You can almost see the wheels turning in their heads as they consider the implications of what you are presenting. They may even seem distracted, but they probably aren't—they are just thinking. Their movements may be quick, but not particularly graceful. Their clothes are usually conservative and more traditional, with a tendency toward primary color choices. They may remind you of the *preppy* type, with a manner that is more formal than friendly.

Thinkers' office environments express their interest in ideas, education, and offbeat curiosities. Their desks tend to be neater and look more organized than average. Pictures of inspiring, historically important places and curious lands that provoke thought are common. Academic diplomas and business charts are a dead giveaway.

Analytically secure with the knowledge that your prospect is a Thinker, you'll be prepared to help her solve the puzzle at hand with a well-thought-out, detailed proposal for your products and services.

The Visualizer Profile: What You See Is What You Get

Last year we got a call from John Macht, President of The Macht Group—a retail and marketing consulting group in Boston—regarding a retail positioning study for Macy's department stores in New England. During an initial phone conversation with John that lasted over a half an hour, he was warm and friendly, absorbing successful business case histories. It became apparent that John was a visual person as he volunteered his own war stories drawn from twenty-plus years of merchandising in the retail industry, including his founding of The Common Market, a chic ahead-of-its-time lifestyle grouping of shops in Westport, Connecticut which he described as "a visual lover's paradise." John said he had seen our column in *ADWEEK*, and heard about our work for other retail clients; he wanted to get together as soon as possible to review our retail capabilities. John added that the purpose of the research was to "help Macy's clearly see the big picture in New England by measuring perceptions of the store and focus on ways Macy's could become more responsive to the needs of the New England population."

A few days later our presentation group traveled into town for a meeting at John's stately quarters. The lobby at his Federal Street office was impressive, with a tasteful combination of artwork and marble. The ride up the elevator was equally impressive with its hand-rubbed mahogany paneling and ornate hand-carved design.

A staff member ushered us into John's office while he was finishing up a phone conversation. A moderately built man wearing trendy eyeglasses, John sat at a beautiful and impressive desk. On the wall were several colorful art prints hung in no particular order. Photos of John and several clients hung randomly on the wall. Other pictures were perched on his desk. Approximately fifteen overlapping piles of papers sat on the floor. Reminder notes were posted here and there. A postcard from Italy was pinned to the wall.

John was a natty dresser and clearly a man who was conscious of fashion. His tailored shirt, sophisticated print tie, and colorful breast-pocket handkerchief were nicely coordinated. John's stylish herringbone suit looked very expensive. His fashionable Barney's raincoat was hanging on the back of his door. Even the rich dark red leather briefcase next to the desk was an eye-catcher.

In the middle of his phone conversation, John eyed the author's new cashmere jacket. Putting his hand over the phone momentarily, he asked, "What kind of fabric is that, cashmere? I like it." Then he returned to his discussion. As he talked, he seemed absorbed in thought, looking up at the ceiling or out the window with an almost blank stare. He wrapped up his phone conversation with an "Okay. I'll see you later."

John smiled, reached across his desk and shook our hands. His handshake was fairly firm. As he spoke his eyes focused with sparkle and intensity. He said, "I'm glad you guys could come in so quickly and give me your point of view on this project. We want to make a quick decision on a research firm so we can get going as soon as possible. I hope you brought some samples of your work for me to review. I will also need some client references."

As the author opened his briefcases and pulled out several research studies, John flipped through the reports quickly, stopping only to observe several graphs and charts. His eyes caught the corner of a colorful brochure from Louis Boston—the world famous men's clothier—hanging out the side of a Louis research report. He asked to see it and then proceeded to scan the brochure page by page. Finally, he mused, "I like what I see and I want your candid perspective on the research we need, particularly the competitive situation, but it's difficult to explain it. If you have some time today, I'd like to take you on a competitive store check right now, so I can show you what is happening. You've really got to see this firsthand visually to understand what's happening."

We got the assignment, and later, after the study had been completed, John observed, in true Visualizer fashion, that "An accurate picture of the competitive scene is essential to long-term success in our business."

John was clearly a Visualizer with great taste. It's not surprising that he was mentioned in flattering terms in the unauthorized Martha Stewart biography, *Just Desserts*. He was in the Visualizer profile the day we saw him, and it was crystal clear from his surroundings that this was his usual profile. To make the Visualizer profile easier to understand and remember, think of Walt Disney, who is seen by many to be one of the most famous, creative, and prolific visual artists of the twentieth century, as well as an extra-

© Disney Enterprises, Inc.

ordinarily successful businessman. His work revolutionized the use of animation in motion pictures, and brought a highly sophisticated sense of visual presentation to the art of storytelling.

Visualizers look at the world from a wide-angle viewpoint. They notice things that others don't see. They are practical, intuitive, and very quick to see things as they are. They see many things at once and are strongly influenced by first impressions.

Visualizers are quick to react. They can absorb a lot of information quickly, particularly if it is visually presented. They will make decisions without undue hesitation if you show them the information they need.

Visualizers are friendly and typically have a wide circle of friends and acquaintances. They work well with other people and in teams, without having to be the leader or the loner. They are aware of the feelings of others, but don't get carried away by sympathy. Their approach to business is decidedly practical. They can bring a fresh new creative viewpoint to a business situation. Many excel as COOs or in operations management.

Visualizers like to talk about seeing, looking, noticing, and searching for creative solutions. They are averagely athletic, but often just as happy to watch sports as to play them. Underneath, as the name implies, Visualizers are *visual/spatial* types. They are more sensitive to visual and spatial input than they are to feelings or analytical thinking.

Identifying and Mirroring the Visualizer Profile

Visualizers use straightforward language to describe what they see. Here are key words that Visualizers like to use:

show	watch
see	perspective
look	perception
visualize	quick
picture	fast
focus	immediate
clear	easy
bright	instant
impression	

John Macht used five key words that Visualizers like to use in his opening statement: "We want to help Macy's CLEARLY SEE the big PICTURE in New England. . .and FOCUS on PERCEPTIONS." This clearly indicated that John was in the Visualizer profile.

Mirroring a Visualizer's profile by using phrases like those below will put Visualizers at ease and help convince them that you see clearly how they look at the many facets of the products or services you are discussing, and how they see the world in general. They will start to trust you, and will gain confidence that you can help them. To help obtain a decision in your favor, try phrases like these:

> I see that. . .
> It looks like you need. . .
> I see what you're saying about. . .
> I can visualize the problem you have. . .
> Here's a quick overview. . .
> Our Chief of Operations sees things the same way
>   you do. . .
> When you take a quick look at. . .
> The solution is simple and easy with our. . .

When Visualizers search their memory to access information they tend to look *up to the left or up to the right*, as John Macht did in our interview with him. An easy way to remember this is that Visualizers are visionaries, and visionaries see visions up in the sky, which is where Visualizers look to recall things. (They may also occasionally look straight ahead, but unfocused, when trying to visualize what you just said.)

Visualizers will shake your hand but won't make a big deal of it. Likewise their eye contact with you is usually strong but not intrusive. Visualizers' body types are generally of moderate build and their movements normal. They like to smile, are friendly, more likely to be positive in attitude, less likely to appear worried, and typically have a good sense of humor. Their clothes are often striking in color or style, but may not be well coordinated. They move easily and quickly from one topic to another, and are not concerned about the logical development of a sales presentation. Details can bore them, so you are better off presenting multiple sales points than dwelling on a few in detail.

Visualizers' office environments express their interest in what they see. Their desks tend to have lots of stuff spread out on them so they can see everything at once. Snapshots of family, office events, and other personal topics fit in alongside other colorful pieces.

When you see clearly that your prospect is a Visualizer, you'll be prepared to quickly show her an overview of what you have to offer, with many colorful pictures and examples of your products and services.

Determining Buying Profiles

You've probably already figured out what your own dominant or primary buying profile is. Most salespeople find it easy to recognize what their primary buying profile is from the language they use as well as many of the other clues outlined. You've probably also thought of clear examples of people you know who primarily fit the other profiles. Recognition of prospects' buying profiles is the key not only to building their trust and confidence, but also to selecting the sales arguments they will respond most strongly to. You can start building your awareness and ability to determine prospects' buying profiles immediately by listening and watching for clues at every sales call you conduct, starting now!

Buying Profile Tracking Strategies

Of the various tracking cues presented, the words people use are usually the easiest to track, and words are the most obvious cue if your prospect changes buying profiles in the middle of an interview. So continuing to pay particular attention to the words and phrases people use will pay off for you.

If you have trouble determining what buying profile your prospect is in from the words or other cues presented above, there are two things you can do. The Commander and Thinker buying profiles tend to be more distinctive and easier to spot than the Visualizer profile, and people in general are less likely to be Commanders or Thinkers than Visualizers. So one thing you can do if you're not sure which buying profile your prospect is in, is to assume he is in the Visualizer profile until something leads you to believe otherwise.

Reverse Profiling: When All Else Fails

Another thing you can do to determine a prospect's buying profile is what we call "reverse profiling." People in the three different profiles react more positively to different categories of sales points and arguments. Chapters 7 through 10 cover in detail which categories are most persuasive to which buying profiles. If you take note of your initial sales presentation points that gain the most positive response, you'll have a good indication of which profile your prospect is in, and you can follow up with more sales points from the categories that are most appealing to that profile. In fact, our own initial sales presentation uses arguments from all three profiles so we know better which profile to pursue in depth. The exceptions are **feature = benefit** sales arguments, because although they appeal best to Visualizers, they have fairly general appeal across all three profiles.

Moving Beyond Trust and Confidence

Once you've determined your prospects' buying profiles, you can use the right verbal and body language to build their trust and confidence—to convince them that you are both on the same wavelength. Then you're ready to determine what buying step your prospects are on, and what arguments in favor of purchasing your product or service will be most persuasive. We cover that next.

Walk the Walk:
The DREAM Buying Path,
Why People Don't Buy,
and the Five Proven Steps
to Success

*If you don't know where you're going, any road
will take you there.*

TED LEVITT[2]

So NOW YOU can talk the talk, and your prospects are listening to
you and liking you because you're listening to them and talking
and moving like they do. Basically, they like you and listen to you
because you sound like your mind works like theirs. Now the
question is, *what are you going to say?* How can you take your selling
power to the next level? How can you *really think* like they do?
How can you walk the walk with them down the buying path
they intuitively take to make a final purchase decision in your
favor? To do that, you need to know why they *don't* buy.

The sales books and courses you are already familiar with or
have heard about typically show you a certain path to follow to
make a sale. Here are two typical paths:

> Building trust ➜ identifying needs ➜ presenting
> solutions ➜ confirming and closing the sale[3]

or:

> Establishing rapport ➤ arousing curiosity ➤ presenting units of conviction ➤ defusing objections ➤ asking for the order 8 ways[4]

Some approaches concentrate on a single aspect of the sale like *Sell the Sizzle, Not the Steak, The Hot Button Approach, The Sale Begins When the Customer Says No,* or *Nine Ways to Close a Sale.*

These different approaches have one thing in common: they present a path to follow from the *salesperson's* point of view. They show you a path that you try to get your prospect to follow. Ultimately you end up trying to *push* the prospect into buying. While these techniques can be valuable in terms of helping you present yourself favorably and develop a professional presence, they don't tell you *what's going on in the prospect's mind.*

We all know that everybody in sales, marketing, and advertising is dying to sell people things, and we're all trying to figure out why people will buy things. What's missing are the real reasons why people *don't* buy things. The old saying in sales mythology is that if somebody has a hidden objection in her mind, and you don't smoke it out and resolve it, then you'll never make the sale. As Lee Dubois, one of the foremost sales trainers in the business, said to us one day, "Salespeople put too much emphasis on closing the sale. If you remove the objections up front the sale closes itself." It's absolutely true. You've got to find out why people don't buy things to eliminate prospects' objections before they get in the way of closing the sale. That's a key to what Buying Path Selling is all about.

Why People Don't Buy

Again, here are the five steps in the DREAM buying path:

D DO step
R REPEAT step
E EVALUATE step
A ACCESS step
M MONEY step

Now let's look at the reasons people *don't* buy at each buying step.

The DO Step: Doing Nothing

When you look at buying things from the prospect's point of view, the first thing you realize is that whatever solution your product or service provides, your prospect is either unaware of the solution or believes the problem has already been solved in some other way. Here are the most frequent reasons we've found through our research for why people do nothing.

Not Aware They Have a Problem: Back Office Body Odor

Way back in the 1920s in the United States (though still true in many other parts of the world), bad breath, body odor, unshaven body parts, and aging shirt collars were not considered problems. These were viewed as normal parts of life. Since then, the invention of "halitosis," "B.O.," "5 o'clock shadow," and "ring around the collar" have convinced millions of people that they actually do have a problem. These inventions have sold zillions of dollars of mouthwash, deodorant, razor blades, and detergent.

In the workaday business world, nobody thought they needed a computer until IBM sold them on the idea that they had a "back office" problem of manual clerical work that would overwhelm them and eat up their profits as they tried to expand.

The plain fact is that if you try to sell solutions to people when they don't believe they have a problem, you are just blowing smoke as far as they are concerned. So the first thing you need to do is determine if they believe they have a problem, and if they don't, convince them that they do. We cover how to do this and all the other "doing nothing" situations in chapter 5.

Unaware Solutions Are Available: The World of Two Left Shoes

Ollie Wight, the founder of the Oliver Wight Company, started his career as an IBM salesman selling an IBM mainframe software system called MRP, short for Manufacturing Resource Planning. MRP (now MRP2/JIT) is a sophisticated planning, forecasting, scheduling, purchasing, and inventory control management system designed to help manufacturers optimize their production operations. For instance, a typical manufacturing problem is partly finished inventory sitting on the factory floor, costing money every minute, waiting for the right parts to show up. If the finished product will be a $100 million dollar airplane and the missing parts are a couple of special $50 hydraulic hoses, the manufacturer has a serious problem. MRP eliminates these kinds of problems. Ollie formed his company to help manufacturing companies purchase and install MRP systems, and to train their people to run them. Ollie and his company became the leader in the field of MRP.

When we asked Ollie to identify the biggest problem in getting people to buy MRP systems, he explained, "The problem with manufacturing people is that they live in a world of two left shoes. . .they know it hurts but they assume the problem can't be fixed any better than they handle it now." The way they handled it in the past was to run around "expediting" parts by swiping them from one project to use them on another. Expediting didn't really solve the problem, but they thought it did. Ollie showed them that expediting merely transferred the problem from one place to another, and that only MRP could actually solve the problem for good. Ollie's genius was to identify the real reason people weren't buying MRP and to attack that reason forcefully. That's how the Oliver Wight Company became the leader in the MRP field.

Unaware That Available Solutions Will Work for Them Because:
"My business is different"

MRP prospects who had heard about MRP and understood how it worked in various types of manufacturing situations had another problem. Even though they knew about MRP and believed it worked for other businesses, they assumed it didn't apply to them because their business was "different." So they ignored it. They suffered needlessly, assuming that their business was so different that no solutions to the problem were available. We run into this same reaction while selling marketing research all the time. Everyone thinks *their* business is different. Prospects feel that just because your stuff works in some other business doesn't mean it will work for theirs.

"If It Ain't Broke Don't Fix It" or The Solution Could Be Worse Than the Problem

How many people have bought a new refrigerator when the old one still worked "just fine"? That all depends on how you define "just fine." If your prospects think their stuff is just fine, you won't get anywhere until you demonstrate convincingly that it isn't.

A related problem is the fear that the solution may be worse than the problem. For instance, the primary difficulty of selling new versions of existing software is the perception that while the new version promises exciting new features, it may also gobble up huge amounts of memory, create problems with the user's existing software and utilities, and even cause bizarre new and potentially catastrophic problems. On top of that there's the aggravation of learning how to use the new version advantageously.

The Windshield Wiper Problem

Procrastination is wonderful. It gives you the satisfaction of having figured out how to solve a problem without the risk or bother of actually having to solve it by taking action. We've all heard various versions of this story:

> A farmer and his nephew were playing hearts at the kitchen table as a rainstorm raged outside. Water leaking through the roof fell into pans and buckets placed strategically around the room. "Uncle," said the nephew, "are ya thinkin' that maybe you oughtta get up on that roof and patch them leaks?"
>
> "Not just yet," the farmer said without looking up from his cards. "It's raining too hard just now."
>
> By the next morning the storm had given way to blue skies. The farmer and his nephew strolled outside after a big breakfast. "Uncle," said the nephew, "I'd be glad to help ya if you wanna fix that old roof today."
>
> "Much obliged, boy, but it ain't leaking no more."

Procrastination is particularly attractive when the problem tends to disappear after a period of time. How many of you are driving a car whose windshield wipers are in perfect shape? Not many hands raised. And we all know what happens. The only time you really notice that the windshield wipers don't work properly is when it's midnight, it's raining like crazy, and all you want to do is get home safely. You wake up the next morning and the sun is shining. What's the first thing you do? You rush out to the nearest gas station and buy new windshield wipers. . .right? WRONG! Because the problem has disappeared until the next time. So the problem and the potential solution don't share the same timing. Procrastination is a powerful method for *doing nothing*.

Phantom Horror Stories: Misinformation and Mistaken Assumptions

Maine Windjammers is an association that represents businesspeople in Camden, Maine who operate half- to two-week sailing vacations aboard their two- and three-masted schooners. These are big, majestic boats that are wondrous to see under sail. Many can handle up to twenty-five passengers. The association approached us to find out why so many of the people who contact them—even after receiving a brochure—never sign up for a trip.

When we interviewed a sample of these *lost prospects*, we uncovered strong negative perceptions of what a sailing vacation would be like. The idea of bobbing about in the ocean and out of sight of land for up to two weeks was considered too solitary and boring for many. Prospective customers envisioned bouts of seasickness and possibly periods of danger. These perceptions corresponded poorly with the reality of the Windjammer sailing experience. First, the schooners are coastal cruisers and almost never out of sight of land; they stop at a port every night and at an island or other land location for most midday lunches. As for the perils of the sea, anyone who drives in New England is safer aboard one of these schooners than he is out on the road.

The mistaken assumptions of these prospects were so strong that huge numbers of potential customers were being lost to other vacation destinations. And the loss of business was due in large measure to misinformation and mistaken assumptions that the boat owners were not fully aware of.

Doing nothing is often the most critical, and the most stubborn buying step to deal with. If you pass by this step in the buying path without being sure that your prospects are ready to seriously consider buying your category of products or services, you will almost certainly fail to make a sale. Chapter 5 shows you the most effective ways to convince prospects to *do something* as opposed to *doing nothing*.

The REPEAT Step: Locked In to the Competition?

If your prospects are already buying your category of products or services from several other vendors, you may have a repeat loyalty problem. If they are only buying from one competitive vendor, you almost certainly have a repeat loyalty problem. You already know how to find out whether they are buying from other vendors. If they are, the question is how do you get them to buy from you?

This sales situation is often frustrating. If you talk the talk, they are listening to you and liking you, and you already know they buy your category of stuff, but they apparently don't have any intention of buying it from you or your company. They are polite but unresponsive to your presentation. You can't seem to get them excited or involved. They are locked into a loyalty cycle that won't quit. Salespeople often make one of two crucial mistakes at this point.

Mistake #1: Attacking the Wrong Buying Step

Mistake number one is trying to overwhelm your prospects with the basic competitive advantages your stuff has over what they are buying now—your product is faster, stronger, easier, bigger, better on a one-to-one comparison basis. They are listening but they aren't buying it.

Mistake #2: Taking It Personally

Mistake number two is taking the rejection personally, and assuming that *you* are the problem. That may be the case, but why would they appear to be listening to you and liking you if you are the problem? So don't rush out and load up on Listerine and Right Guard. Odds are that buying from *you* isn't the problem, buying your *company's* products and services is.

The Two Real Reasons: Satisfaction and Risk Aversion

The real reason for brand loyalty is almost always a combination of real satisfaction with the status quo, and a reluctance to change. Changing suppliers almost always exposes the buyer to some degree of real or imagined risk, hassle, or expense. "The devil you know is better than the devil you don't know."

It stands to reason, as our research clearly shows, that to get prospects out of their repeat cycle or "loyalty loop," you must do two things:

1. Create a credible doubt that continuing to use the same brand is acceptable behavior.
2. Reduce their risk of changing to your brand.

As you'll see in chapter 6, there are a number of key arguments that can create doubt about staying with their current brand, and persuade your prospects to risk changing to you as their new supplier.

The EVALUATION Step: Not Convinced?

The Evaluation step occurs when your prospects have already decided to do something, and aren't locked into a repeat cycle with another supplier. Therefore, they are willing to evaluate your stuff with a reasonably open mind. Far and away the single most common reason for losing a sale at the Evaluation step is that you are using the wrong arguments. Not just the wrong specific arguments, but the wrong buying profile category of arguments. Your sales training has no doubt given you a slew of arguments that might or might not be effective in persuading a random prospect that your stuff is the greatest. But when you get to the point of making a presentation to a particular prospect, you have no idea which arguments are likely to be more persuasive and which ones less. So you run down your general list of arguments and you hit some and miss some. If you get lucky, you may hit it off early and feel you're having a great day. If you try out what prove to be a couple of losers with this prospect right off the bat, you are already in trouble and the selling gets harder and harder instead of easier and easier.

The problem is you're using a list of arguments that, more likely than not, doesn't match how your particular prospect makes evaluation decisions. In fact, your list of arguments is most likely to be the list that's most persuasive to *you*, but the odds that your prospect is in the same buying profile as you are is only one out of three!

Wrong Buying Profile = Wrong Argument

Sales literature is filled with advice on how to present sales arguments in the most persuasive manner. But no matter how persuasive your presentation technique, if you are presenting arguments that your prospects don't relate to, the reception will be lukewarm at best. For instance, you may be presenting to a Thinker using Commander arguments that are persuasive to you, but less than persuasive to the prospect. Or you are presenting to a Visualizer but get tangled up in a numbers grid that only a Thinker could love. And so on and so on.

Here's where your knowledge of prospects' buying profiles can do double duty. When you know their profile, you not only know how to Talk the Talk and get them listening and liking you, you can also Tell the Tale by selecting the specific evaluation arguments that you know have the most persuasive power. Here are some examples of why prospects don't buy what you have to say in the Evaluation step.

Commander Turnoffs

Commanders often get bored with complex number charts like spreadsheets that don't make an obvious point. And they usually find long strings of logical reasoning and fine detail unpersuasive as well. Commanders want *action*, and they want to know where you are in the action. If you don't tell them and they don't bother to ask, you'll get a cold reception. They subscribe to the dictum, "No battle plan ever survived contact with the enemy," attributed to Karl von Clausewitz, Germany's most famous general. But don't be fooled into thinking Commanders are anti-intellectual. Rather, they are strongly pro-action. Chapter 8 shows the categories of sales arguments that are most persuasive to Commanders.

Thinker Turnoffs

Thinkers, on the other hand, are not impressed by things like market dominance or other signs that you are winning the battle. Their response is often that market leaders tend to be lazy, self-serving, and sometimes bordering on the unethical. They are interested in the facts in significant detail, and if you don't have the factual details, you can easily lose their confidence in you and what you are selling. Signs of disorganization or a scattered presentation will also put them off, as will imprecise language. Excessive talk does not impress them either—as "Dragnet's" Sergeant Joe Friday used to say, "Just give me the facts, ma'am, just the facts." Chapter 9 shows what kinds sales arguments are most persuasive to Thinkers.

Visualizer Turnoffs

Visualizers will look at anything for a short period of time, but you better keep the interview moving. They like lots of input, but want you to do the work of showing them what it all means. Fast is good, slow is bad. Complex charts, like undigested spreadsheets, can give them mental indigestion. Pictures, including numbers in graphic form (pie charts, bar charts, moving lines, and so on) are preferred. Chapter 10 shows the types of sales arguments that Visualizers like best.

The ACCESS Step: Will You Deliver on the Promise?

If your company distributes a product or service that is sold by other competing distributors, will your prospects access it through you? It can be heartbreaking when you've convinced your prospect to buy your brand, only to lose the sale to a competing distributor of the same or very similar product. Price is always a consideration (see Money step that follows), but it's rarely the only consideration. To make and keep the sale, it is critical that you make access to the product comfortable, easy, and risk-free—through you and your company.

In fact, price aside, our research shows that the broad category of sales service and customer service is most often the key reason in deciding which competing vendor, supplier, or outlet to eliminate from consideration. It becomes more important as you progress from the "long list" of potential vendors to the "short list." In study after study, our research has shown that salespeople are the key to making or breaking the sale at the Access step on a prospect's buying path.

Slow Response

The quicker you can respond, the better your chances of closing the sale and keeping the business. What your prospect and particularly your customer want to know is that you are "on the case." A classic example is the research we did for Shipley Chemicals, now part of Rohm & Haas. One of the keys to their success was that a majority of their customers felt they were superior to their competition in these three categories:

- ➡ Responding to problems
- ➡ Knowing how and where to get help for you
- ➡ Having a sense of urgency

Notice that the emphasis is more on the speed of response than on the speed of solving the problem. Communication and a positive attitude are key.

Salesperson Knowledge and Expertise

When was the last time you went out to buy a car at a respected dealership and got a salesman who insisted on telling you everything you didn't want to know, but you bought it from him anyway? Probably never. You most likely either came back later and talked to a different salesperson, tried a different dealership, or possibly even talked to the sales manager and asked for a different salesperson. As a salesperson, your product knowledge and expertise only work for you if you're selling what the prospect wants to buy. During our research for an automobile manufacturer, we "shopped" dealer salespeople to find out which ones did the best job at selling the latest models. The winners of the contest were consistently the ones who asked just enough questions to use their product knowledge and expertise to sell what the prospects really wanted to buy.

More Than Just Good Salesmanship

The preceding problems basically relate to poor salesmanship, and the only way to fix them is good sales training, good sales supervision, and quality control feedback. But beyond basic solid salesmanship is the question of what *specific arguments* to use to make sure you get the sale instead of a competitor who sells the same product or service. Chapter 12 gives you the answers.

The MONEY Step: From Underpriced Suspicion to Sticker Shock

The immediate raw cash price of your product or service is seldom the only purchase consideration unless you are selling pork bellies or other commodities. Ted Levitt, the Harvard Business School professor who turned marketing upside down with his famous article "Marketing Myopia," first published in the *Harvard Business Review* in 1960, claims that true commodity product and service sales are extremely rare.

Interestingly, when we research salespeople and their lost prospects at the same time, by far the most common reason salespeople give for losing a sale is that *the price was too high*. Their lost prospects, however, rarely attribute their nonbuying decisions to price. On top of that, *priced too high* is only one of many price related reasons given for not buying. Prospects give price reasons for not buying that include:

- ➨ Unsupported pricing (includes pricing too low as well as too high)
- ➨ Disappointing value
- ➨ Too risky or questionable an investment
- ➨ Failure to relate pricing to longer term considerations

Buying Signals and Price Expectations

When a prospect suddenly asks "How much does this cost?", many consider this a strong buying signal. It usually is. But it can also be a trap if you don't know what price structure the prospect is expecting.

Research on purchase intent shows clearly that buyers' price expectations vary over a wide range above and below actual pricing. Price expectations that are half to double the actual pricing are common! Pricing expectations vary depending on prospects' knowledge of your product or service and its competition, and their response to the variety of sales arguments that you claim for your product. The odds are, however, that a prospect's price expectations will be slightly to substantially above or below your actual pricing, unless they have already been made aware of your specific pricing.

The further away their price expectations are, *either higher or lower*, from your actual pricing, the less likely they are to buy. And the more important it is to justify your pricing in their eyes.

Real Value, Real Investment, Real Competition

Everyone talks about *value*, it's one of the latest buzzwords, but our experience is that very few salespeople, or marketers or advertising people, really understand what goes on inside prospects' heads when it comes to how they intuitively perceive value. When prospects' perceived values, including negatives such as risk as well as positives, don't equal or exceed your pricing, they won't buy.

Every serious purchase is an *investment* to some degree, bubble gum and pinball games aside. To that degree, the return on investment may be as important or more important than today's price. If you don't prove to prospects that the return on investment meets or exceeds their requirements, there is a serious risk they won't buy.

In the eyes of your prospects, your *competition* may be totally different than the companies and products *you* consider to be your competition. And the comparison prospects make may be unfavorable for you. If it is, you can lose the sale even though they would like to buy your product but *can't afford it* or can't justify it. You need to turn this around by comparing your product to the real competition.

There are lots of reasons people don't buy if they don't like your pricing. It's either too high, or too low, or doesn't present enough value, or doesn't give enough return on investment, or compares unfavorably to what they consider the competition to be. You can change their minds and close the sale, if you know how their minds are working, and use the arguments that will conquer these final objections. Chapter 13 gives you the final steps to closing the sale.

Five Proven Steps to Success

Now that you have considered the variety of reasons why people don't buy, it's time to move on to why they *do* buy. We'll follow prospects through their DREAM path, and show you which sales arguments are most persuasive at each decision step. These arguments will move them along the path to the ultimate decision in your favor, a closed sale.

Each DREAM step does two things. First, each step gives you the key questions to ask to make sure you know which DREAM step your prospects are on. Once you know that, you will know which set of sales arguments to use. Second, each step gives you the most powerful basic sales arguments to use to persuade prospects to make decisions in your favor, based on the DREAM step they are on. These strategic sales arguments are the basic categories or types of arguments. You will probably have a number of specific sales points that fit into any one particular type of sales argument category.

In addition, for the Evaluation DREAM step, there are different sales argument categories that are more powerful for Commanders versus Thinkers versus Visualizers. For each sales argument category, we present at least one example that makes the thrust of the argument clear and easy for you to understand, and helps you build your own specific sales points for your product or service in each category.

In graphic form, the DREAM path looks like this:

The DREAM Buying Path

| Do Step |
| REPEAT Step |
| EVALUATE Step |

| COMMANDER Buying Profile |
| THINKER Buying Profile |
| VISUALIZER Buying Profile |

| ACCESS Step |
| MONEY Step |

What Each DREAM Step Does for Your Prospects

When you make presentations to prospects that follow their DREAM path, you're really doing them a big favor.

You're listening to them and talking to them in language they understand and can easily respond to, not just talking at them in your own language mode, which may be harder for them to understand. You are speaking directly to the decision they need to make at that moment, to move ahead in the purchase decision process. You aren't wasting their time with sales points that don't relate to where they are now in the decision process.

You give prospects your best sales points from the sales argument categories that mean the most to them. These are the arguments they can understand most easily, and the ones they depend on most heavily to make decisions in the purchase process. You don't bore them or turn them off with sales arguments that they don't care about or consider marginal or not to the point.

When it comes down to it, you're selling to prospects the way they want to buy. You are respecting who they are, where they are, and what they need, to make an informed decision. Suddenly, selling becomes a truly interactive process, and you are connecting with your customers in ways that are dramatically more effective than the same old canned sales pitches that are supposed to work for everybody, no matter who they are, where they are, or what they need to make a decision. You are respecting them, and they will respect you and what you have to say.

What Each DREAM Step Does for You

When you use the DREAM buying path techniques, you will know what the most powerful sales argument categories are for each of the five DREAM steps, and when and how to use them. This in turn will give you the opportunity to generate a whole new set of tactical sales points that you never thought of using before. You'll be amazed at the number of new sales points that had never before occurred to you. And you will be able to refine and elaborate the sales points you are already using, placing them in appropriate categories, and using them when and where they are most effective. The number and effectiveness of the tactical sales points at your disposal will increase substantially and will become much more comprehensive.

Now you'll know which sales points to use in each situation. Your prospects will listen to you more closely. They will understand and internalize what you have to say more completely. They will buy more often, and your sales will increase dramatically.

First Things First

The best thing to do right now is to jump into Step 1: DO something, anything, and see how it all works.

Step 1:
DO Something, Anything!

To do nothing is to decide.

Anonymous

IF YOU KNOW your prospects use your category of products and services, you can skip this step and go directly to the Repeat step. But if you don't know, you must find out what their experience has been through questions like these:

I've brought along several examples of our widgets that I feel (I think. . .) you might find interesting. Have you ever purchased widgets before?" (If the answer is *No*), "Have you ever considered purchasing them?" (If the answer is *Yes*), "What was your experience at that time?

These opening questions will tell you if prospects are in the do nothing mode, and if they are, these questions will give you some background as to why they haven't bought. Make sure you start here. You must know whether they have purchased your category of products or services before. Otherwise you're in danger of committing Big Mistake #1.

Are They Ready?

You also need to know how ready prospects are, both personally and organizationally, to move ahead with the purchase process. If you don't know whether they are ready to move ahead, simply get them talking about where they are. People really do like to be listened to.

When we are in doubt, we often pull out a one-inch thick research report, toss it on the table upside down, and ask, "If this was the final report for your project, what would you want it to tell you?" The resulting conversation should give you a clear idea of where prospects are in the purchase process and where the organization stands on the proposed project. If they aren't personally and organizationally ready to move ahead, you must create that readiness.

Deciding to Do Something

Four proven categories of sales arguments can be used to motivate prospects to take action and *do something*. These are tough-minded arguments, but they work just as well when delivered via a soft sell, consultative approach.

The four most powerful *do something* argument categories, ranked in order of effectiveness, are:

1. Create the fear
2. Re-create the pain
3. Focus on the real issue
4. New solution to an old problem

Create the Fear

Inertia is the enemy of action. But inertia is a fact of human life. As we saw in chapter 4, people can think of all sorts of reasons to sit tight and do nothing. But the consequences of not taking action can be negative and serious. For example, the office manager who cannot bring herself to upgrade the vintage PCs being used by the company's managers, customer service personnel, and clerical employees may be damaging her firm's competitive position. "Most of these machines are just used for report writing and creating simple spreadsheets," she objects. "Why pay a lot of money for new equipment to do that?"

The fact is that her old PCs are only used as fancy typewriters because they aren't capable of much else. Meanwhile, the company's main competitor is using newer, faster, more capable machines to save time and money—most of its correspondence is now sent by e-mail; long-distance phone charges have dropped by 40 percent; and documents that used to be sent by overnight air express travel for free as e-mail attachments. Their competitor is also using its new machines to provide better service to field reps and their customers. Its reps can check product availability in "real time" online, and customers can query or place orders directly through the company's Web page. This company is saving money while responding faster to its customer base. And its employees are keeping apace with the technology of the future. Customers perceive this company as effective and really "on the ball." Meanwhile, the company with the tired old machines is stuck in a time warp. That's the danger of inertia.

By alerting your prospects to the potential negative consequences of not taking action, you will be doing them a favor. In the case just cited, the salesperson was a powerful source of important information, explaining how other companies are using new office hardware to be more effective and competitive. You will also be using the strongest sales argument for getting prospects to take action instead of taking no action at all.

● *Listerine: Insidious*

Listerine virtually created the antiseptic mouthwash industry with hard-hitting ads that did a superb job of creating the fear of *halitosis*, their advertising term for bad breath. A July 1935 Listerine ad in *Needlecraft Magazine* reads in part:

> ### Women Men Despise
>
> *There are a half dozen of them in every large office. What does it matter that they are attractive and engaging if they commit the offense unpardonable? Who cares about their beauty and charm if between stands that insurmountable hurdle, halitosis (bad breath).*
>
> *You Never Know You yourself never know when you have halitosis (unpleasant breath). That's the insidious thing about it. But others do, and judge you accordingly.*

Your sales approach may be slightly less alarming than the 1935 vintage Listerine ad, but this argument works well at any level. Following is an example from our own research.

● *P$\overline{U}$R Water Filters: Lead Is the Enemy*
Sometimes it's necessary to educate potential buyers about your product's ability to solve a problem they didn't know existed.

Back when P$\overline{U}$R Water Filters were first introduced, consumers weren't aware of the high lead content that existed in certain water supplies, or the fact that traditional water filters didn't remove it from drinking water. P$\overline{U}$R realized that their unique filter technology (which removed 93 percent of the lead) could not only take market share from other brands, it could expand the market by attracting new buyers who had never purchased any filters at all, but who were fearful of lead and other contaminants. This highly competitive sales approach was used effectively with trade buyers and delivered through consumer advertising in the ad shown opposite.

As Brian Sullivan, Founder and President of Recovery Engineering observes, "During our one-on-one sales calls to retailers, we promoted the fact that, 'Only P$\overline{U}$R filters remove lead and keep

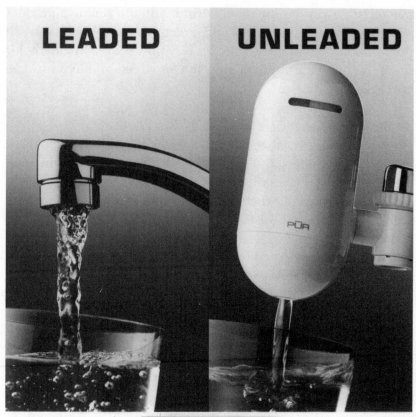

*SHIPPING, HANDLING AND APPLICABLE TAX NOT INCLUDED.

it out of drinking water. However, these days everyone has heard about lead in the water, so we've become more educational about the range of contaminants we remove."

The PŪR Water Filter generated initial attention due to consumers' fear of lead in their water. . .once they realized it existed. As a result, PŪR was able to call attention to itself and capture a leading market share in their key distribution channels.

Re-create the Pain

Another reason for inertia and inaction is that people forget the pain of unpleasant circumstances experienced in the past. And overall, it's a good thing we do. But if you are selling a product that relieves the pain, it pays to re-create the pain before you sell the solution. This approach can be very powerful, particularly for situations that occur infrequently, but for which solutions must be purchased in advance.

● *Vander Zanden: Dying Onstage*

Businesspeople know that public speaking skills can help them advance their careers. But the apprehension and stage fright associated with public speaking are such that most executives would rather not think about them until they absolutely have to prepare and deliver a speech. Just about everyone can recall, with some pain or embarrassment, a trip to the podium that left them feeling like a total idiot! This ad for Vander Zanden Executive Speech-making is a classic at re-creating the pain, and impossible to ignore.

> ### There Are Two Times In Life
> ### When You're Totally Alone.
> ### Just Before You Die.
> ### And Just
> ### Before You Make A Speech.
> Vander Zanden Executive Speechmaking

● *Avery Dennison: Building a Better Mousetrap. . .Out of Plastic*

In the early '90s, Avery Dennison—a leader in the fastener field—had a real sales challenge regarding their Plastic Staple Fastener for attaching size tickets to clothing. Although the product represented a technological breakthrough and seemed like an automatic success, they were having some difficulty convincing several major pants manufacturers to adopt the new plastic staple. Buyers were hesitant to convert to a new Plastic Staple Fastener without more information about how consumers would react to the change. So Avery Dennison commissioned us to conduct consumer research to explore the fastener versus thread issue.

We conducted one-on-one consumer interviews with both male and female consumers, which we videotaped. People were quick to recall the *pain* and *hassle* they had experienced in removing thread-sewn tags. Key problems included damaging new pants or other garments, and even creating holes in them when trying to remove tags with scissors or razors. Consumers were universal in preferring the new Plastic Staple Fastener over thread. It really was a better mousetrap! Here's how Avery Dennison presented it in their trade brochures:

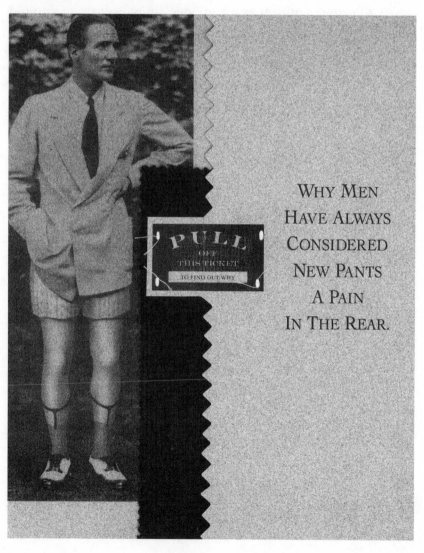

WHY MEN HAVE ALWAYS CONSIDERED NEW PANTS A PAIN IN THE REAR.

The company's sales force shared the research with buyers and in some cases played video excerpts from interviews so the trade could see for themselves that the fastener was a real solution to a painful problem. As a result, trade resistance was overcome and the Plastic Staple Fastener was sold effectively. The research provided new information that convinced buyers that consumers were really *bothered* by the old-fashioned thread tack, and that the Avery Dennison Plastic Staple Fastener offered an excellent solution with no downside risk. Today, the Plastic Staple Fastener continues to grow in appeal as it provides a new solution to an old problem.

Focus on the Real Issue

Sometimes people simply try to solve a problem or tackle an opportunity the wrong way. When they do, they are not focused on the real issue. Your job in this case is to redirect the focus to address the real issue. A classic example is the recent and very successful advertising campaign for Hammermill copier and laser printer paper.

The Hammermill advertisement shows a crumpled piece of paper with the following headline:

> *IT'S NOT THE* **STUPID** *COPIER.*
> *IT'S THE STUPID* **PAPER**.

The ad goes on to point out that most paper jams are caused by the paper, and that "Hammermill copy paper has the stiffness and weight to glide easily through even the fastest copiers." A nice solution to the *real* problem.

● *Arthur D. Little: Whatever It Takes to Get There First*

Our work back in 1990 with Arthur D. Little (ADL), a highly respected technology and management consulting firm based in Cambridge, Massachusetts specializing in new product development, provides an excellent illustration of finding and focusing on the real issue. When we met with ADL executives to review the situation, they expressed frustration at not being able to generate a stronger volume of consulting business in several specific industry groups. Despite the fact that ADL provided an excellent service, one they believed was clearly superior to competitive firms, they had difficulty even getting in the prospect's door to present their philosophy and unique approach, and outline their extensive worldwide resources. It became clear that the obstacle was not other consulting firms, but the disuse of consulting firms in general. In-house new product development was the competition. If ADL could convince them to use outside consulting for new product development, they knew they would open up a big opportunity.

We conducted research among over 100 CEOs, divisional general managers, chief scientists, and other key decision makers to determine why they were not more receptive to ADL sales initiatives. What this sales-based research uncovered was a real eye-opener that provided new opportunities for ADL.

The challenge was finding out what would motivate ADL prospects to use an outside vendor. One of our open-ended, conversational questions was the key that unlocked the puzzle. The wording of the questions was: "What are the three biggest problems facing you in developing successful new products and how are you responding to each one?" The assumption of ADL executives who were involved in the project was that creating the best possible products would be the primary answer to this question, but they had missed something. It turned out that the biggest problem facing companies introducing new products was *time*, not creating the perfect new product.

As one respondent at a Fortune 500 company put it,

> The biggest problems we face in new product development are time constraints. We want good products that perform well, but not overly engineered products that take forever to develop and make us a Johnny Come Lately. The money is in being there first and that's why time is so critical. If a company like ADL can convince us that they have the professionals and philosophy to compress the time cycle, then we're all ears.

So time was the critical real issue. We also learned that some of the firms who had never worked with ADL perceived the company as being big, and thus potentially slow. This perception existed despite the fact that ADL had intentionally unbundled itself years earlier and had created small "lean and mean" teams for each project, comprised of experts who were already up-to-speed in each client's category, and who could speed up the development of new products, not slow them down. The time issue became so important that ADL coined a new phrase, "time effectiveness," which it used to supplement "cost effectiveness."

ADL did not need to change the way it did business. It just set out to change prospects' perceptions of what it did. And when it approached prospects with an emphasis on speeding up the time cycle, it hit a responsive chord. According to one ADL insider, "It's much easier to get appointments to see prospects when you focus on the real issue. It also helped correct any misconception that ADL could not speed up new product entries."

● *Massachusetts Medical Society: Putting the Cap on Malpractice Premiums*

During the mid-'80s we were asked to help the Massachusetts Medical Society gather information regarding what the *Boston Globe* termed, "The Malpractice Crisis." Consumers were suing doctors so frequently that doctors were fleeing the state. The *Globe* reported, "Although doctors continued to win most malpractice trials in Massachusetts, the number of verdicts for the plaintiff rose from three a year to fourteen; and the average jury award increased from $75,000 in 1980 to $485,000 in 1985. As a result, the underwriters' total pay-out jumped from $5.3 million in 1980 to $42 million in 1985." State legislators were aware of the problem, but didn't consider it a problem that resonated with consumers.

The research we conducted among consumers showed that they felt the two parties to blame were the lawyers pushing clients to sue, and consumers suing when they really shouldn't have. The research also revealed that consumers felt they would ultimately end up paying for the increased premiums, and that a physician shortage would occur if something wasn't done. Universally, they believed that the legislature should act to set caps on malpractice awards, or else the problem would never be resolved.

Here are the consumer results. Throughout the book, you'll see the research results for many of our examples shown in this type of format indexed for easy reading.[5] We usually show three statements, the winner, the loser, and an average statement in the middle. An index of 100 would be exactly average. Most results of our research are shown on an index basis, whether we were testing a product, a service, or an idea. For example, the following chart shows that consumers were 53 percent more likely than average (153 index versus 100 average) to be concerned about their health care costs increasing due to frivolous malpractice awards. Conversely, consumers were 70 percent below average in believing that physicians were "blowing the whole thing out of proportion" (30 index versus 100 being average.)

Massachusetts Medical Society

Question: "Why do you think there should be caps placed on malpractice awards to consumers?"

Buying Index

The increased costs of physician malpractice
   insurance premiums will be passed on to
   consumers ....153 winner

The supply of doctors may decrease.........................106

Physicians cannot afford to pay higher rates.............30 loser

Note: An index of 100 is an average response. Research was conducted in 1986 among 400 consumers residing in Massachusetts.

W&W's top line research findings were released and eventually, following the adoption of a litigation cap, premiums began to level off, then decline by 25 percent. Five years later a headline in the *Globe*'s Business Section declared, "The End of the Malpractice Crisis."

New Solution to an Old Problem

It's great to have a truly new solution to an old problem. It's even better if you have an old product that turns out to be the new solution to an old problem.

● *Arm & Hammer: Out of the Oven and Into the Fridge*

One of the classic revivals of an old product is the case of Arm & Hammer Baking Soda. For years and years, Arm & Hammer Baking Soda was (and still is) the number one baking soda in America. Back in the early 1900s, being the number one baking soda was great, because American women baked at home a great deal. Then home baking started to decline, and Arm & Hammer sales declined along with it. Until someone (we don't know who) discovered that if you put Arm & Hammer Baking Soda in the refrigerator it would reduce the odors inside. The advertising campaign promoting the use of Arm & Hammer Baking Soda in the refrigerator was incredibly successful and launched the company into a frenzy of multiuse advertising campaigns and then into line-extension product introductions such as Arm & Hammer Laundry Detergent and Arm & Hammer Toothpaste.

The Arm & Hammer story is unusual, because most new solutions to old problems are, in fact, new products. One such new product was the Shower Massage by Teledyne Water Pik, which provided a new solution to an old problem.

● *Shower Massage: "Feels Good Because It Reduces Hot Water Usage"*

Back in the early '80s Teledyne Water Pik faced a challenge. It had sold 4.5 million units of its Shower Massage, but was experiencing a slowdown in sales. Research indicated that the key to influencing purchase of the product was getting consumers to take a Shower Massage shower once. . .because the unexpectedly pleasurable experience sold the product. The challenge was getting consumers to try the product the first time. How do you give away a free Shower Massage shower?

Dick Bruno, VP of Marketing & Sales, came up with a brilliant solution one morning as he took a shower at a hotel while on a road trip. As his shower suddenly turned cold, Dick realized that a hotel's greatest fear is running out of hot water in the morning. The problem becomes most apparent when the front desk lights up with complaints from irate guests. Shower Massage offered a solution by reducing water consumption (hot and cold) by three quarters. Armed with this data, Dick approached the Holiday Inn, Sheraton, Marriot, and Hilton hotel chains with the potential benefits of reducing hot water consumption, and an offer they couldn't refuse: a special $10 unit price (versus $40 consumer price). It worked! Hotels loved it. They could provide a guest benefit while conserving hot water. And Shower Massage could generate broad trial usage, the key to future growth for the brand. Within two years, 30 percent of consumers who bought a Shower Massage said it was due to trying one at a hotel or motel. Within four years one out of every four hotels and motels in America had Shower Massages. Shower Massage's successful sales approach capitalized on an old problem by offering a very different new solution.

● *Connected Online Backup: Relieving That Free-floating Anxiety*

Do you use a computer? Do you "back up" your work on a regular basis by copying it to a floppy disk, or a backup tape or a safe separate hard disk or similar device? You probably do. But you may not feel entirely comfortable with your backup procedures.

Connected Corporation learned through sales research that small to midsize companies harbored a lot of free-floating anxiety about backing up computer files. At first glance, it looked like everyone backed up their computer files all the time:

> "Do you currently keep backup copies of your computer files?" Yes: 95%

But a closer inspection of the research showed that daily backup was low:

> "Do you back up your computer files on a daily basis?" Yes: 27%

And fears about losing data abounded:

> "What is your greatest fear about losing computer files?"
> Having to re-create/rekey the data 37%
> Lost time 26%
> Lost data 25%
> Other fears 33%

Connected Corporation came up with a brand new solution to this old problem and called it COB, the Connected Online Backup system. The COB system, based in Framingham, Massachusetts, automatically calls up your computer and backs up your data to multiple COB security sites. You can access the system to retrieve data any time from anywhere, and you get a CD-ROM of every backup each quarter.

The COB system has lots of advantageous selling points, but the big question at the time of its introduction was, "Which are the most persuasive?" By knowing the best selling arguments in advance for this new solution, the COB sales force could focus on the advantages of the new solution and push the right buttons during the selling process. We tested ten selling propositions. Listed below are the winner, the loser, and one in the middle.

The Connected Corporation

Question: "In your opinion what's the best reason for using this new method of backing up your company's data?"

	Buying Index	
Fast and automatic backup	192	winner
Every change and revision is saved	107	
The system has three levels of security	38	loser

Note: An index of 100 is an average response. Research was conducted in 1993 among 400 business prospects nationwide.

The COB system has become the leader in the field in just a few years because the company is focusing their sales efforts on the strongest appeals, and delivering a great service. As David Cane, Founder and President of Connected Corporation said, "With a new product you have to know how to sell it right the first time or you can go broke trying to figure it out. We gained success and a leadership position by knowing how to sell it right the first time."

It's Yours to Keep

Once you have convinced your prospects to Do something, the odds are in your favor that you'll get the sale, because you were the first to get them to see the light. But don't take this for granted. You'll need to nail them down with some units of conviction from the Evaluation step, and seal it with Access and Money arguments.

Chapter

6

Step 2: Breaking the REPEAT Cycle

The devil you know is better than the devil you don't know.

FOLK SAYING

YOU KNOW THAT your prospects are ready to purchase wangledangers, you know whether they've purchased them before, and you've asked them what their experience was. Don't take the short answers, because the more you know about their prior experience with wangledangers, the better you'll be able to handle the Repeat step. You'll find most people are pleased that you're interested in their experience, or total lack of it, and are easily forthcoming.

Subtle probing on your part should reveal what prospects' sophistication level is in your product category, whether they have purchased or influenced the purchase of wangledangers for their current employer, and how strong their relationship to their current supplier is, if any. In our own business for instance, the personal experience of most clients with research has been limited to focus groups, though a few have had extensive prior experience, and relationships with other research suppliers.

If prospects don't appear to have significant prior relationships, you can skip the Repeat step and go to the Evaluation step and sell your stuff full steam ahead. If they do appear to have significant prior relationships, you must attack this point before moving on.

Failure to attack the repeat cycle will produce polite head nodding and the dreaded response: "Can you leave me some material for my files?" Thus you will be committing Big Mistake #2.

Why They Don't Buy: Big Mistake #2

If you assume they are willing to consider switching their loyalty to another supplier, and they aren't, you'll be using the *wrong sales arguments*, and you will likely fail to get a decision in your favor. You must create *doubt* in their minds about the wisdom of their loyalty.

As we mentioned briefly in chapter 4, you have two ways to attack the Repeat step. You can:

1. Create credible doubt about the wisdom of the prospect's current purchasing choice.
2. Reduce the apparent risk of switching to you as a supplier.

These are actually two sides of the same coin for any Repeat argument. The stronger the prior relationship, the more the risk of continuing that relationship needs to be stressed; the weaker the relationship is, the more the opportunity to achieve better results should be stressed.

Choose Your Arguments

The five most powerful argument categories against repeating, ranked in order of effectiveness, are:

1. Hidden risks revealed
2. Hassle-free alternative
3. Raising expectations

4. Don't be outdated or old-fashioned

5. Do it right, not over

Hidden Risks Revealed

A "hidden risk" is anything associated with a competing or alternative product that could do damage to prospects or their business. Poultry producers, for example, have always enjoyed hinting at the purported health risks associated with their dinnertime rival, red meat. In the late '70s, the banking industry sponsored an ad campaign aimed at stemming the tide of defections from passbook savings accounts to higher-yielding money market funds. "That house could have been ours," a mournful couple confessed—a beautiful suburban house with a "Sold" sign in the background. The implication of the ad was that this couple had lost their down payment money when they moved their hard-earned savings from their bank to (though never stated) a money market fund. "It seemed so safe," the husband droned lamely.

Revealing a hidden risk gains its power from the element of surprise. But it works even if your prospects may have suspected or even have knowledge of the hidden risk, because it compliments them on being smart enough to have suspected or uncovered it.

● *Amoco: Not Hazardous to Your Car's Health*

Sometime after the great gas crunch of the '70s, Amoco gasoline ran an ad with a headline that looked suspiciously like a cigarette pack warning label. It read:

> *Warning: Major Car Manufacturers*
> *Have Determined That Gasolines*
> *Containing Methanol May Be Hazardous*
> *To Your New Car's Health.*

The ad went on to reassure car owners that Amoco gasoline was a safe solution because it contained no methanol, a cheap ingredient added to some gasolines.

Exposing the hidden risks of buying from the competition can be a very powerful way of breaking a prospect's repeat cycle.

● *PŪR Water Filters: A Healthier Approach*

This argument for PŪR water filters is a first cousin to the one described in the previous chapter: creating fear. There we described the initial success enjoyed by PŪR Water Filters for exposing lead and other contaminants in the water. But our subsequent buying index research also indicated that the public viewed the possibility of *backwash* from a saturated filter as a real risk.

PŪR Water Filters

Question: "Which aspect of the PŪR Water Filter makes you most interested in buying this filter versus other filters on the market?"

Buying Index

PŪR's red Automatic Safety Monitor alerts you
    when the filter is used up...219 winner

Fully guaranteed...105

It uses the same technology proven effective
    by outdoorsmen and explorers
    worldwide...42 loser

Note: An index of 100 is an average response. Research was conducted in 1993 among 300 consumers nationwide.

As the only manufacturer whose product automatically turned itself off when the filter was used up—thus preventing the *backwash* of contaminants from an overful filter—PŪR was able to capitalize on the *hidden risk revealed* argument. The Automatic Safety Monitor is sold with strong results both in the trade and consumer markets.

According to Tom Angelis, Senior VP of Sales and Marketing in 1993,

> The sales based research uncovered the importance of PUR's unique patented Automatic Safety Monitor, which assures healthier water. We entered the faucet mounted category that was twenty-five years old, with a significantly more expensive product ($49.95 versus $14.99) and were still able to capture a 50 percent market share in twelve months. The key was our ability to sell the primary

selling benefit to both the consumer and the trade, but with a different spin for each group.

With consumers, the ASM filter turned itself off, alerted the user, and prevented backwash. The trade was approached with a different selling strategy, but the message still used the automatic shut-off ASM filter as the differentiator. Other filters get changed by consumers only three times a year because people forget. With PŪR it's impossible to forget because it turns itself off and alerts you when it's used up (on average six times a year). What this means to the trade is upscale customers returning twice as often to repurchase PŪR filters. Our sales guys showed the research results to trade buyers and proved the appeal of an automatic shut-off filter, but we didn't stop there. We showed the trade how the PŪR filters would bring back customers more often and proved that our filter was more profitable than the low priced version. We sold profitability and productivity per square foot. We trained buyers to look at our selling advantage: profitability per square foot, not unit sales. In fact I remember one time proving that three PŪR water filter facings would generate more bottom line profit than six toaster oven facings.

That's how the exposé of the *hidden risk* of backwash contaminants in common water filters, and the ability of the PŪR ASM to

PŪR PLUS
Self-Monitoring Water Filter.®

Our best filter provides the greatest protection from contaminants.

Eliminates Cryptosporidium and Giardia.

Reduces 98% Lead, 98% Chlorine, 99% sediment.

Now, PŪR Plus also reduces 85% Mercury, 97% Lindane, 97% Atrazine, and significantly reduces Asbestos.

Eliminates bad taste and odor.

FM-3000 includes one microfilter.

Each microfilter provides 2 to 3 months of healthier, great tasting water for less than 18¢ per gallon.

eliminate this risk, turned into a powerful selling argument to both the consumer and the trade.

Hassle-free Alternative

Almost every competitive product or service has something about it that can create a hassle at some point during its purchase or use. Sometimes the hassle can be a real problem. At other times, a buyer's hesitation is just the fear of an unknown hassle. Levi Strauss handles this problem for their Levi's 501 jeans like this:

IF YOU HAVE A PROBLEM WITH COMMITMENT, THERE'S A MONEY-BACK GUARANTEE.

501

ORIGINAL 501 BLUE JEANS   LEVI STRAUSS & CO.

Subway sandwich shop has an irresistible guarantee: "Take one bite, and if you're not satisfied, you'll get your money back." Talk about putting your money where your mouth is! The mail-order business was built on the basis of money-back satisfaction guarantees and they certainly help in many other cases as well. But there are other equally strong ways to make a sale hassle-free. Oftentimes your company does things that make for a hassle-free switch that have never been used before as a prominent part of the sales presentation.

● *Lappen's Auto Parts: Losers Keepers*

Lappen's Auto Parts used research successfully to defend itself from major competitors like Pep Boys and NAPA. This research uncovered a powerful new offer for do-it-yourselfers that took the hassle out of buying, and most importantly, took the hassle out of returning auto parts: "Lifetime warranty on parts, *even if you lose the receipt.*" The consumer research looked like this.

Lappen's Auto Parts

Question: "What makes Lappen's Auto Parts more appealing than other stores where you purchase auto parts?"

Buying Index

Every part Lappen's sells has our lifetime warranty, *even if you can't find the receipt*!...142 winner

Our lowest prices around are guaranteed. 103

We're number one with professional mechanics. ....32 loser

Note: An index of 100 is an average response. Interviews were conducted in the Boston metropolitan area during 1995 among 250 males who do their own automobile maintenance and repairs.

As one customer put it,

> Who wants the hassle of looking for a receipt to take a part back? This offers peace of mind knowing they will replace it without a receipt and without making me feel like an idiot. This would be enough to make me shop at Lappen's exclusively.

Lappen's tells us that this unique offer has been highly effective in increasing its business despite new inroads from major competitors. According to Ed Lappens,

> Every member of our staff, from the guys at the front counter to the telephone operators and parts delivery personnel has made it his mission to inform the public of our new policy. At first, people can't believe it. They wonder what the gimmick is, but after we explain how our new free Power Card permits our computer system to assign every order to a specific customer for future reference, they become believers. It has not only solidified our customer base and made them more loyal, it's attracting new customers, who love us for it. We're no longer selling parts, we're selling peace of mind.

● *Marvin's Window of Selling Opportunity*

Minnesota-based Marvin Windows & Doors provides a great example of a company that has used a no-hassle complete service program to increase sales.

In a national trade-oriented sales research study conducted among builders and remodelers, we tested ten selling propositions and learned that despite the fact that Marvin offers an incredible selection of over 10,000 standard-size windows, plus virtually any custom window imaginable, current and prospective clients were more keen on service than manufacturing. What really gets the attention of builders and remodelers is Marvin's commitment to supporting them: fixing problems and overcoming any obstacles in order to help their clients get the job done right. As Victoria Vogt, Marvin's Research Director is quick to point out, "This includes doing whatever is necessary to deliver the windows when promised and having a dedicated 'problem solution team' always ready to answer questions, provide architectural support, and deal with any problems in the field even if that means a rush trip to the job site."

Marvin's complete service promise speaks directly to builders'

Marvin Windows & Doors

Question: "What is there about Marvin that makes buying their products more appealing than buying from the competition?"

	Buying Index	
Complete service provided before, during, and after the job	156	winner
Uses the finest quality materials	96	
Over fifty years experience	24	loser

Note: An index of 100 is an average response. A total of 400 professional builders and remodelers were interviewed nationwide during 1995.

and remodelers' fear that a late delivery of windows will throw a job off schedule, resulting in disgruntled clients, penalties, and probably lost income. The promise appeals to the "engineer hat" worn by every client during the job because *time is money*. Our research revealed that when Marvin's customers force themselves into their "engineer" (Thinker) role, critical financial questions surface such as, "Now that I've sold it, how long will it take to get the job done and what's my liability if I fall off schedule?"

As Tom Angelis, Marvin's VP of Marketing observes, "Sure we've gotta make a product that's top quality, but our customers want to know, 'What else can you do for me to make my job easier, keep me on schedule, and help me make a buck?'"

Raising Expectations

Prospects who are comfortable with the status quo may not have thought about opportunities to do better. They may be setting their sights too low—settling for second best. You can break prospects' current purchasing patterns if you can get them to raise their expectations for value or service.

Whenever you see an Avis car leasing ad, or even the buttons worn by the Avis counter personnel, you'll still see the Avis slogan *We Try Harder*. This famous advertising campaign was launched three decades ago amid much controversy. The original headline read:

> *When you're only No. 2, you try harder. Or else.*
> *AVIS*

This Avis campaign has been spectacularly successful, and the secret to its success had two sources: (1) It raised buyer expectations of what great service could be; (2) It was based on something that people believed intuitively.

- *Blue Cross/Blue Shield: A Healthy Approach to Purchasing Health Insurance*

Blue Cross/Blue Shield of Rhode Island once asked us to investigate how people make decisions regarding their health plan selections. We found consumers go through a three-phase process in selecting a plan: (1) The selection of the doctor(s), (2) The selection of the plan which has the doctor, and (3) The selection (or inheritance) of the hospitals offered by the plan. The research showed that the *widest selection of physicians* was the winning hot button. It clearly raised the expectations of what you could get in a health plan.

Blue Cross/Blue Shield

Question: "If you were thinking about switching health plans, what would be the key reason(s) for switching to Blue Cross/Blue Shield of Rhode Island?"

	Buying Index
Widest selection of physicians	164 winner
Costs less than other plans	107
Pays claims promptly	61 loser

Note: An index of 100 is an average response. In 1990 a total of 550 consumers and business owners were interviewed in Rhode Island.

Once Blue Cross/Blue Shield realized the importance of physician selection, they were able to generate sales and advertising programs for their HealthMate program that delivered the key benefit to both business and consumer prospects. Their corporate sales staff specifically focused their selling stories around their comprehensive physician lists. Their billboard (see below) delivered the physician story with high impact:

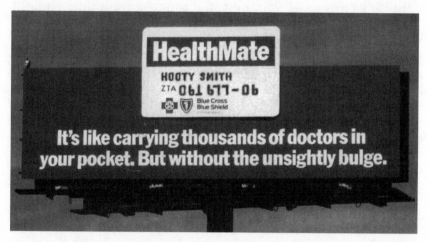

The results indicated a strong increase in businesses offering Blue Cross/Blue Shield to their employees, as well as a strong increase in consumer choice of Blue Cross/Blue Shield among competitive plans. On top of that, it helped the ad agency, Pagano Schenck & Kay, capture a major *best of category* advertising award.

● *Odd Job Stores: The Secret of the Closeout King*

We're all familiar with the *closeout* stores, where you can get stuff that didn't make it to the first-tier retail shops. The quality of the merchandise in these establishments varies widely, from last year's models to insurance salvage. In New York, Howie Snyder has changed all that, and made himself the King of Closeouts by raising people's expectations about what they can find at his chain of Odd Job stores.

In 1997 Odd Job had 30 retail stores in New York City and surrounding areas, but was experiencing a flattening of sales. Our research showed that while current customers were *wild* about Odd Job and shopped there at least twice a week, noncustomers viewed Odd Job as just another closeout company with irregulars, damaged goods, liquidations, and so on. In fact, Odd Job is nothing of the sort; it specializes in first quality brand name merchandise.

The research suggested that the way to raise sales was to raise consumer expectations about what they would find at any Odd Job store. One way to do that was to spell out the company's philosophy about merchandise quality and pricing. The result was "Howie's Pledge"—a very personal promise from the owner of Odd Job stores to his customers.

HOWIE'S PLEDGE

1. I will offer first-quality brand name merchandise which I would be proud to bring home to my family.

2. I will buy right so I can sell to my customers at *below* original wholesale.

3. The sale isn't over until the customer takes it home, uses it, and is happy with it. This is honored by Odd Job's 15-day "no hassle" money- back guarantee.

Howie's Pledge effectively raised consumer expectations about Odd Job's merchandise quality. Further, it promised low prices and a guarantee as good as any high-priced department store. This clearly set Odd Job apart from the typical liquidator. Research indicated that Howie's Pledge had a much more powerful impact on prospective customers than the company's prior *Closeouts With Class* advertising.

When the campaign was introduced, every teller wore a Howie's Pledge button. Howie's Pledge was displayed in stores, and a Howie's Pledge flier went into every customer's shopping bag. This campaign created tremendous word-of-mouth advertising as current customers spread the word about Odd Job's unique philosophy to friends and family members.

According to Howie Snyder,

Howie's Pledge was proof right at our stores that we are different. Then, when we promoted why Odd Job was unique as a closeout company it woke people up because it

"A Dollar Saved Is A Dollar Earned"

Odd Job Founder

raised their expectations. People didn't expect a closeout company to offer first-quality merchandise or back it up with department store return policies. It got consumers to visit us once and that's all it takes to make them believers.

Don't Be Outdated or Old-fashioned

Some people respond strongly to the suggestion that they may be behind the times in their thinking about your product or service category. For example, here's the headline from an ad that appeared in *Wired* magazine for the NewsPage Web site:

> *Are you still getting your news from dead trees?*
> *http://www.newspage.com*

A modern up-to-date solution to an old problem is an effective way to sell your products whether they are cars or computers.

● *How Detroit Beat the Old-fashioned Foreign Cars*

Between the mid-'60s and the mid-'80s, Detroit was under assault from foreign competitors, including a bevy of luxury imports, particularly the Lexus, Infinity, and Mercedes.

As part of its selling effort, one of the U.S. automakers' luxury car divisions asked us to do some research on its own salespeople. It wanted to know how effective its salespeople were in positioning its own models against the foreign cars that were out to capture the same customers. We tested this by sending our own people out to the client's dealerships disguised as prospective buyers.

As a first step, we developed a Sales Force Rating Sheet covering five critical selling areas. Then our crew of mystery shoppers interviewed a cross section of the sales force to measure their selling tactics and determine where they might be missing opportunities. Here's the rating sheet we used.

**Mystery Shopper
Rating Sheet Questionnaire**
Specific Area 1-10 Ratings:

☐ **1. Quality:** Is this car's quality any better than it was a few years ago?

☐ **2. Power:** Is this car really fast? How much acceleration and passing power does it have?

☐ **3. Handling and Wheels:** How well does it handle? What kind of tires does it have?

☐ **4. Safety:** What safety and anti-theft features does it have?

☐ **5. Foreign competition:** Specifically, how does it compare favorably to Lexus, Infinity, or Mercedes?

The results showed that although our client's sales force had done an excellent job preparing to sell the new models, they were selling against their traditional U.S. luxury brand competitors, not the exotic new entries from abroad. Their thinking was locked in past experience. While the salespeople understood the features and benefits of their own products, they were missing opportunities by failing to sell against the new upscale imports that represented the real threat.

We reported that: "Only a few salespeople fell into the trap of selling on lower price when asked why their automobile represents a 'better buy' than the foreign cars. No one made the mistake of 'knocking the competition.' Instead, they focused on brand strengths. What they really need, however, are more reasons why their line is more advanced than the new foreign competition."

Most salespeople had some general information regarding their car's strengths versus the foreign competition, but few had specific competitive knowledge on key areas of difference (e.g., front-wheel drive versus the rear-wheel drive used by some foreign models). More training was needed to get our client's salespeople really geared up against the foreign competition. And surprisingly, most salespeople did not mention that the brand had won a Malcolm Baldrige Award unless they were specifically asked "What outside recognition has your automobile received?" Even then, many salespeople cited auto magazine reviews or editorials, not the Baldrige Award, despite the fact that it was posted prominently at the point-of-sale exhibit.

Armed with new sales training that showed how their advanced design and engineering made many foreign models old-fashioned and outdated, our client was able to successfully defend itself from further erosion of sales.

Do It Right, Not Over

Poor decisions are costly. Nobody likes to make the wrong purchase decision then have to correct it. FRAM Oil Filters has used this simple fact of life to create a high level of visibility for itself and its products. For years, it has been selling consumers on the benefits of paying slightly more for top-quality oil filters. Its television spots feature an auto mechanic who offers a clear choice:

> ## "Pay Me Now or Pay Me Later."
> ## FRAM Oil Filters

The solution, paying him now for a FRAM oil filter, will be far less expensive than the cost of a new engine. This type of selling strategy can be very effective in motivating people to do something *right, not over*. The same selling strategy works as well or better in the business and industrial area as it does in the consumer sector.

● *Data Instruments: Don't Get Your Hand Caught in the Wringer*

Data Instruments approached us back in the '70s with a sales challenge. The company had developed an advance in safety equipment, the Shadow 1 Safety Curtain, which automatically turned off a potentially dangerous machine if a worker's body interrupted the infrared safety field. But prospects were slow to convert from traditional devices such as "pull backs," due largely to price constraints. At the time, a Presidential Task Force was putting pressure on many industries to meet tighter OSHA safety requirements and was creating new opportunities for Data Instruments. What Data Instruments wanted to know was what would be the most powerful sales arguments to accelerate a prospect's switch from existing technology.

Research showed that the best way to motivate change was to convince potential buyers that if they didn't change over to the new safety products now, sooner or later they would just have to replace any traditional safety equipment with the new technology anyway.

Industry publications were supportive of the trend toward upgraded safety devices, so Data Instruments decided to aggressively pursue key magazines such as *Metal Stamping* for endorsement articles. It worked. Favorable articles were generated. Armed with reprints, the Data Instruments sales force was able to create conviction and overcome buyer resistance to change. As Ed Colbert, CEO of Data Instruments, put it, "When a salesperson could show prospects that their favorite trade publications endorsed our technology, it helped get them to do it right, instead of having to do it over again later. Consequently, we were able to carve out a major segment of the safety market early on, which has helped us maintain leadership today."

The Goal: A Level Playing Field

If you want to break the repeat purchase cycle and become your prospects' new supplier, you have to create doubt in their minds—doubt that they are doing the right thing. This chapter has shown you four ways to do this, and how to make your own offerings a hassle-free alternative.

No matter which method you use, you have to break the repeat cycle. If you fail, you'll get the usual polite brush-off. But if you succeed, you will have created a level playing field. And you'll be halfway home. Once you have a level playing field, prospects will be willing to evaluate your story, which is our next step.

7

Step 3: Tell the Tale
The Three EVALUATION
Buying Profiles

If it looks like a duck, walks like a duck,
and talks like a duck, it's a duck.

OLD MAINE SAYING

ONCE YOUR PROSPECTS have decided to do something, and they've decided that they are willing to seriously consider you as a new supplier, they are really ready to listen to what your product or service is all about.

You already know how to Talk the Talk with these prospects by communicating in their intuitive language. You have Walked the Walk with them through the Do and Repeat steps to the point where they are ready to Evaluate what you have to offer. This is your golden opportunity to convince them that what you have to offer is superior to any other choice. But how can you take maximum advantage of this opportunity? How can you Tell the Tale with the greatest impact?

Did you ever notice that different kinds of people seem to respond to different kinds of sales arguments? Of course you have. That's part of the fun of selling. But it's not much fun if you're not winning. Imagine what it would be like if you always knew what kinds of sales points, examples, and demonstrations would score best with each prospect you talked to. You could double, even triple your effectiveness, and avoid those difficult times when you know you aren't connecting with your prospect.

Here's what it would be like. Jon Goward, a master at creating television commercials, recently asked us to test three of his thirty-second TV commercials for Cape Cod Tourism. He wanted to find out which one had the greatest impact and why. We suggested showing each commercial to about twenty people who had vacationed on the Cape in the past, but hadn't visited recently. We'd interview each one separately, to find out which commercial scored best.

One of Jon's commercials showed people enjoying typical Cape Cod physical family activities, including swimming and bicycle riding. Another focused on the calm, quiet, solitary pleasure of being away from the rat race and city life. His third spot zoomed in on the visual beauty of the Cape. We and Jon and four of his clients sat behind the one-way mirror in a screening facility to watch the twenty minute one-on-one interviews. The three commercials were shown about halfway through each interview.

Before the interviews started we made a friendly bet with Jon. We bet him that we could *guess* which commercial would be most persuasive to each respondent within *thirty seconds* of when each respondent walked into the interviewing room. We also bet that we could *outguess* him, no matter how much time he took. Of course, Jon took us up on the bet.

For us, this bet was like shooting fish in a barrel. We got nineteen out of twenty right! Jon got eight right, no better than random guessing. When it was over, Jon was astounded. After all, he was the one who had created the commercials.

"How did you do that?" he asked. You know how we did it. We picked up on the early cues that let us classify each respondent as being in a Commander, Thinker, or Visualizer profile. Then we predicted that the Commanders would pick the "swimming" commercial that had lots of physical family activity, the Thinkers would pick the cerebral "get away from it all" spot, and the Visualizers would pick the "beauty" spot. After all, when a heavyset guy dressed in a Red Sox baseball cap and a Celtics t-shirt says "I feel like I should be driving the family down to the Cape right now," you *know* he's going to go for the swimming spot. If you were a travel agent and you wanted to sell this guy a Cape Cod vacation, you'd *know* which set of pictures to show him and which *sales points* to make. You would know how to Tell the Tale and *win the sale*.

Telling the Tale is the heart of Buying Path Selling. This chapter will show you how to take what you already know about your prospect, and use that knowledge to focus on the specific kinds of sales arguments that will have the greatest impact at the most critical Evaluation decision step. You will be presenting your sales story in the best possible way for each individual prospect. Your sales effectiveness will dramatically increase, and selling will become more fun.

Three Buying Profiles: Three Types of Sales Arguments

You already know how to identify your prospect by buying profile. She's responding as a Commander, a Thinker, or a Visualizer. By mirroring her spoken and body language you have gained her trust and confidence. She has decided to do something, and is willing to consider what you have to offer. Now that you know which buying profile she's in, you also have the key to which sales arguments will be more persuasive to her, because certain sales arguments appeal more to Commanders, others to Thinkers, and still others to Visualizers. If you can't wait to find out what appeals to each type, skip to the end of this chapter right now, but return here later because the rest of this chapter is key to helping you remember which sales arguments work best with which profiles.

Something Old, Something New

Amazingly, the basics of planning and delivering a persuasive speech to different types of people was first formulated and taught as the art of rhetoric about 2500 years ago during the Golden Age of ancient Greece! Development of this art grew out of an important need in the newly created Greek democracies, especially in Athens and Syracuse. There, citizens put a high value on the ability to participate in the political life of their city-state by speaking in public on the important issues of the day. Philosophers, generals, and politicians were intensely interested in methods that would make them more persuasive and more able to devastate the arguments of their opponents. Pericles, Socrates, Plato, and Aristotle were all accomplished in the art of rhetoric. The study of rhetoric continued as a key element in Western education until very recently. Today, ironically, in an age of mass literacy, newspapers, radio, and television, most political discourse has been reduced to ten-second sound bites.

The greatest attribute of Greek rhetoric was the discovery that different kinds of people respond to one of three different types of arguments used in proving a claim. The three basic categories of classic rhetorical arguments are:

1. *People*-oriented arguments, particularly regarding *reputation*
2. *Logical* arguments, including maxims, syllogisms, and sayings
3. Visual observances of *objective facts* including analogies to nature, preferably combined with *emotional appeals*

If an ancient Greek had to deliver a speech to a broad audience—which would likely contain people who responded differently to different arguments—he made sure that he provided arguments and examples that would appeal to each type.

These three categories of Greek rhetoric have continued to be used from ancient to modern times. For instance, many classical rhetorical passages occur in the New Testament of the Bible, particularly in the Gospel of Luke, as Luke was highly educated in the Greek tradition. An example of a complete classical rhetorical argument, including all three categories, can be found in the following passages from Luke 11: 9,10[6]

(Primary claim:) One should not worry about life (food) or body (clothing).

(Logical reason:) Life is more than food and the body is more than clothing.

(Objective fact/emotional appeal:) Ravens do not work for food; God provides for them. You are worth more than the birds.

(Logical reason:) No one can add a day to life by worrying.

(Objective fact:) Lilies do not work, yet are clothed.

(People/reputation:) Solomon in all his splendor was not as magnificent as the lilies.

(Objective fact/emotional appeal:) Notice the grass. If God puts beautiful clothes on the grass, won't he put clothes on you?

(Restatement of claim:) One should not worry about food and drink.

(People/reputation:) All the nations worry about such things.

(Call to action:) Instead, make sure of God's rule over you, and all these things will be yours as well.

A modern sound bite example incorporating each of the three argument categories is found in the political litmus test offered by rivals during the 1992 presidential campaign for determining whether a proposal was simply a tax cut in disguise.

"If it looks like a duck (visual), walks like a duck (physical/personal), and talks like a duck (logical speech), it's a duck."

The three basic types of arguments are clearly reflected in the three buying profile argument categories we will describe in chapters 8 through 10. But the objectives of classical rhetoric and modern salesmanship are quite different. Classic rhetoric was devised to persuade an assembled audience of different kinds of people through the act of public speaking. In contrast, modern salesmanship is concerned primarily (but not exclusively) with persuading one person at a time, most often through face-to-face interaction. Something new is needed to meet the modern sales objective. *We need to know which specific categories of arguments are likely to be more effective with each individual prospect we meet.*

Although classic rhetoric was first developed 2500 years ago, these three categories continue to surface in modern scientific studies of neuroscience, psychology, psychotherapy, modern sales technique, and our own sales- and marketing-based survey research.

Modern Neuroscience: Left Brain, Right Brain, Midbrain

Classical rhetoric's enduring power may be explained by the way our brains operate. Brain surgeons and researchers have discovered that different human capabilities reside in different areas of the brain. Some of these areas are physically quite small and functionally very specific. Overall, however, the human brain appears to be divided into three general areas. You may have heard about "left brain/right brain" thinking. Both are very important and quite different parts of the puzzle. But you may not have heard of midbrain thinking, which turns out to be as important as the left and right brain functions.

The Midbrain

The left and right brain areas actually sit on top of this quite different part of the human brain. The midbrain originally developed over 100 million years ago in reptiles, and has continued to grow and evolve in mammals including humans. It is believed to be the key to sophisticated survival thinking, including:

- Friend or foe identification
- Fight or flight decisions
- Hunting and territory defense

- Family, social group, and team formation and organization
- Cooperative leadership behavior and development

It controls or processes many emotional responses, including pleasure and pain, social and sexual attraction, fear, anger, and feelings of confidence and trust versus distrust. In very general terms, the midbrain seems to deal with the types of concerns that are important to Commanders.

The Left Brain

The *left* hemisphere of the brain sits on top of the midbrain on the left side, and is associated with the right eye and right hand. For most of us, it provides a number of functions including:

- Logical, rational, linear, and analytical thinking
- Speech production
- Time and sequence orientation
- Mathematical thinking

When you concentrate on solving a math or logic puzzle, you are probably using your left brain. Again, in very general terms, the left brain appears to deal with what's important to Thinkers.

The Right Brain

The *right* hemisphere of the brain sits on top of the midbrain on the right side, and is associated with your left eye and left hand. For most of us, it provides a number of functions including:

- Two-dimensional visual and three-dimensional spatial thinking
- Nonverbal intuition
- The ability to deal with multiple inputs creatively
- Holistic, non-sequenced thought processes

When you come up with a new solution that's "outside of the box," you are most likely using your right brain. The right brain appears to deal with what's important to Visualizers.

Neuroscience has proved, as we would expect, that we use all three basic areas of our brain to some degree most of the time. But given a specific activity to concentrate on or deal with at a specific time, one of the three areas will likely be working harder than the other two. We suspect that this effect appears because a prospect is in a Commander, Thinker, or Visualizer profile.

Cognitive Science

Cognitive science is a relatively new term for examining more closely how the human mind really works. Initially sparked by the MIT linguist Noam Chomsky, who argued that human speech must be generated in part by rules and procedures that are built into the human brain at birth, cognitive science has expanded rapidly to elaborate various theories of how people use different parts of the brain to perform different tasks. Marvin Minsky, also from MIT, contends in his book *The Society of Mind*, that the mind is more like a debating society than a monolithic structure.[7] Daniel Dennett of Tufts University asks, in his book *Consciousness Explained*, what we mean when we say "That wasn't the real me talking last night."[8] If it wasn't the real you, who was it? And Stephen Pinker, also from MIT, argues persuasively in his new book *How The Mind Works* that the mind works by using many different mental "modules" to do different tasks.[9] In sales, we want to know which module or modules our prospects are using to evaluate what we are presenting. If we know that, we can present the sales points that are more persuasive to them at that time.

Multiple Intelligences

Harvard's Howard Gardner is considered the foremost proponent of a theory of the mind called "Multiple Intelligences." His basic position, as detailed in his landmark book *Frames of Mind*, is that human intelligence is much more diverse than the dimensions of intelligence measured by standard IQ tests.[10] Human intelligence is, in his view, a combination of at least seven intelligences. These intelligences are sufficiently distinct that they can be observed and measured separately. Five of these seven intelligences can be matched up with our three buying profiles.

Gardner's Seven Intelligences	Wallace & Washburn Three Buying Profiles
Bodily-kinesthetic	Commander
Interpersonal (knowledge of others)	Commander
Logical-mathematical	Thinker
Linguistic	Thinker
Spatial-visual	Visualizer
[Musical [Intrapersonal (knowledge of self)	Less important for decision making

While Gardner's concerns as a leader in education and intelligence theory include human developmental potential in *all* the arts and sciences, our concerns are concentrated more narrowly on how people make decisions, particularly purchase decisions. From our perspective, the Commander profile appears to be related to a combination of bodily-kinesthetic and interpersonal intelligences. The Thinker profile seems related to logical-mathematical and linguistic intelligences. Finally, the Visualizer profile appears to relate to Gardner's spatial-visual intelligences. The correspondence is certainly not one-to-one, but seems directionally strong. (The musical and intrapersonal intelligences seem less important with respect to purchase decision making.)

Neuro-Linguistic Programming

We covered Neuro-Linguistic Programming, or NLP, earlier, in chapter 3. NLP is another way of looking at how people's minds work, particularly in personal decision making. With NLP as a starting point, we have expanded the techniques for identifying which profile prospects are in, and have shown how to mirror prospects' verbal and body language to create trust and confidence. The combination of NLP and insights from neuroscience and multiple intelligence theory led us to test which kinds of arguments were more effective in persuading prospects in each of our three profiles. Here's what we found.

Matching the Sales Arguments to the Profiles

During the past twenty-three years, we have tested over five thousand sales and marketing arguments in over five hundred business and consumer studies. Since 1988, when we first formulated Buying Path Selling analysis, we suspected we had a pretty good idea of which sales arguments were more effective for each particular profile, and we've used Buying Path Selling in this form very successfully. But in 1997 and early 1998, we decided to do some new quantitative research to test exactly which arguments are most persuasive at each DREAM decision step, including which arguments are more powerful for Commanders, Thinkers, and Visualizers at the critical Evaluation step.

We reviewed every study we conducted since 1976 to uncover the sales arguments that were repeatedly the most persuasive in each of the DREAM steps. This is the basis for the material presented in each of the DREAM step chapters, including the DO and REPEAT chapters you've just read, and the EVALUATION, ACCESS, and MONEY chapters coming up. But then we went a step further.

We conducted surveys among hundreds of respondents, covering both business prospects and consumers, for client surveys and our own proprietary studies, to nail down which evaluation sales argument categories appeal more to one profile than the other two. For instance, the Commander buying profile list below shows which arguments have greater appeal to Commanders than they do to Thinkers or Visualizers. The lists are then ranked in order of impact:

Commander Buying Profile

1. Strength, durability, toughness
2. Years in business
3. Proven and time-tested product
4. #1, Dominant in sales or market
5. Famous clients, famous founder

Thinker Buying Profile

1. Best future results
2. Logical design
3. Best procedures
4. Clever, unique, design
5. Endorsed by Experts

Visualizer Buying Profile

1. Clear features = clear benefits

2. Best-looking design

3. Quick and easy

4. Cosmetic appeal

These findings can help you make the strongest possible impression on individual prospective customers.

A Technique That Works

Combine the three buying profiles model with effective matching sales arguments and you will have a first-class ticket to dramatically increased sales. This method of selling appears to be related to human brain development and organization, but we don't claim to prove it. It seems to be related to the theory of multiple intelligences, but it's not a theory of how the brain works. It is a powerful extension of the NLP model, but it goes beyond NLP because it focuses on which specific categories of sales arguments people find most persuasive.

The three buying profiles model may be as different from how the brain actually works as IBM's Deeper Blue chess playing computer program is from Grandmaster Gary Kasparoff's brain. But Deeper Blue can *win*. And just like Deeper Blue, the more you use the Buying Path Selling program, the more you'll win. That's what's important.

The important thing about any model is how well it works in the real world. The three buying profiles model works. It works for us and it will work for you. As Nike says: "Just Do It."

The next three chapters offer a wealth of examples on how to use the Evaluation sales arguments that are more persuasive for each buying profile.

8

The Commander Buying Profile: Heavyweight Arguments

It's not what you know, it's who you know.

Anonymous

YOUR PROSPECT IS in the Commander profile, and he is ready to seriously evaluate your products and services. You're ready to Tell the Tale the way a Commander wants to hear it when you understand the five most powerful Commander arguments.

What a Commander really wants to know is who you and your company are. One of the great business ads from McGraw-Hill Magazines shows your most formidable Commander type prospect, a heavyset, mean old man staring at you, saying:

> *"I don't know who you are.*
> *I don't know your company.*
> *I don't know your company's product.*
> *I don't know what your company's product stands for.*
> *I don't know your company's customers.*
> *I don't know your company's record.*
> *I don't know your company's reputation.*
> *Now—what was it you wanted to sell me?"*
> McGraw-Hill Magazines

Sales Arguments for Commanders

McGraw-Hill hit many of the Commander's key ways of evaluating you and your company's products and services. Our research shows that five argument categories are more powerful for Commanders than Thinkers or Visualizers in the Evaluation step. They are, ranked in order of effectiveness:

1. Strength, durability, toughness
2. Years in business
3. Proven, time-tested product
4. #1, dominant in sales or market
5. Famous clients, famous founder

Strength, Durability, Toughness

Products that have great strength, durability, and toughness last a long time. Everyone would like to have their automobile last longer than it does, and Volvo has developed a strong reputation for durability. In a classic advertisement they stated their position very clearly:

> *How often do you buy
> a new car?*
>
> *That's too often.*
>
> VOLVO

● *Eastpak: Guaranteed for Life, Maybe Longer*

Guarantees are just one way to dramatize this point and make it concrete. Eastpak illustrates the power of the guarantee.

Eastpak—a major competitor in the backpack field—has taken durability and toughness all the way to the bank. Our research for them confirmed the value of a "Lifetime Guarantee Which You Probably Won't Need To Use." One of their best ads (opposite) shows a skeleton in the desert wearing an Eastpak backpack. The headline reads, "Guaranteed for life. Maybe longer."

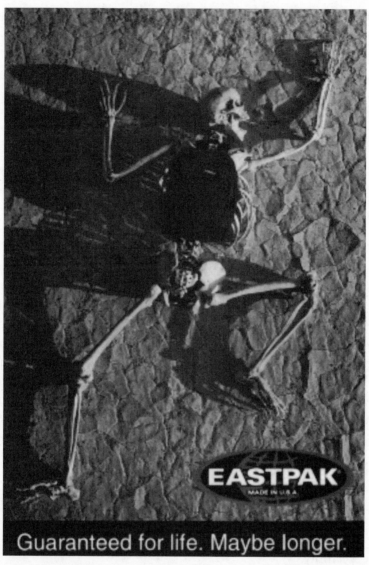

Guaranteed for life. Maybe longer.

The nationwide sales study we did for Eastpak among trade buyers confirmed that quality was even more important to trade buyers than product turnover, delivery, styling/design, or even profitability. It also revealed that backpack trade buyers were extremely receptive to Eastpak posters and brochures if they illustrated quality. In no time, the Eastpak sales force was swamped with requests for posters and collateral materials promoting Eastpak's quality. The company's use of fine quality stitching, stress point reinforcements, Cordura, functional design, and waterproof fabric gave it the confidence to offer the lifetime guarantee.

Eastpak

Question: "What would make you most receptive to stocking Eastpak and recommending it to your customers?"

Buying Index

Strength, durability, and toughness
    backed by a *lifetime guarantee*..........................204 winner

Value to the consumer..94

Products are advertised to consumers.........................59 loser

Note: An index of 100 is an average response. A total of 200 trade interviews were conducted nationwide during 1987.

As a result of the research, the sales team made maximum use of Eastpak's strength, durability, and toughness, as backed by the Lifetime Guarantee. They were able to focus on what was important to trade buyers as well as consumers and avoid wasting time on sales points that were less relevant. Today, Eastpak is a major player in the backpack market and continues to emphasize durability and its guarantee. Commanders are particularly receptive to this type of argument.

Years in Business

If your company or product has been around a long time, it's a strong selling point to Commanders. Levi's 501 jeans have *really* been around a long time. One of their recent advertisements says it very simply.

BORN BEFORE TRENDS EXISTED.

501

ORIGINAL 501 BLUE JEANS   LEVI STRAUSS & CO.

But Zildjian Cymbals has been in business even longer than Levi Strauss & Co.

● *Zildjian Cymbals Since 1623*

Commander types are impressed by how many years you've managed to be in business, not just that you're doing well today. When we conducted research for Zildjian Cymbals among established and more mature drummers, many of whom were professionals, there were some big surprises. Of the ten selling arguments we tested, ranging from, "Zildjian is the # 1 cymbal in the world," to "Zildjian Cymbals are made using a secret formula which has been passed down from one family member to the next over the years," none came close to the selling proposition that "Zildjian has been around since 1623." To everyone's surprise, the fact that Zildjian *uses a secret formula* was not a runaway winner among drummers. It scored only in the average range.

Zildjian Cymbals

Question: "What is there about Zildjian Cymbals that makes you more likely to buy that brand over the competition?"

Buying Index

The original name in drumming since 1623 ....200 winner

Uses a secret formula...104

Zildjian: When you want to treat
　　yourself to the best ....22 loser

Note: An index of 100 is an average response. A total of 300 drummers were interviewed nationwide during 1989.

While the musical instrument segment has nearly flattened, Zildjian has continued to increase market share and grow at a double-digit pace. As Colin Schofield, VP of Marketing Worldwide Sales puts it, "We realize that while having the hot young bands using Zildjian is important to younger drummers, we also know that with all the confusion created by new cymbal manufacturers entering the market, many drummers look for a solid brand with tradition and heritage."

● *Hathaway: Shirtmakers Since 1837*

Hathaway Shirts also discovered the importance of business longevity. Our research among current and potential Hathaway customers underscored the importance of Hathaway's heritage to its target group (upscale males age 40+). The "Since 1837" line scored so well (see box) that the company used it in its advertising and direct selling. It even began printing this powerful endorsement on every shirt bag! (Talk about putting the trigger on the package!)

Hathaway Shirts

Question: "What aspect of Hathaway make you most interested in buying the brand?"

	Buying Index
Since 1837	167 winner
The oldest shirt company in America	102
Made in Maine	33 loser (except in Maine)

Note: An index of 100 is an average response. A total of six focus groups were conducted among 62 male prospects in the Northeast during 1996.

Management fully realized the importance of their heritage and encouraged the sales force to take every opportunity to inform trade prospects that Hathaway is "The oldest shirtmaker in America. . .since 1837." In fact, while most shirt companies are looking for the latest trends in terms of design, Hathaway is placing added emphasis on classic, all-American shirts called the Hathaway Classic, which are full fitting and comfortable. This new direction toward the past, not the future, has helped Hathaway's sales force to revitalize the brand and exceed sales projections.

Proven and Time-tested Product

Proven, tested products are particularly appealing to Commanders. And it helps if a company can show an unusually interesting proving and testing situation. DuPont did just that with their Quallofil thermal lining for sleeping bags and other cold weather gear. One of its ads shows a mountain climber hanging off an icy cliff, with this headline:

> ## The sleeping bag that cold can't conquer.
> ### Filled with DuPont Quallofil and proved on Mt. Everest.

Hopefully you won't have to go to Mount Everest for proof. In fact, your prospect may already be aware of your reputation, but needs to be reminded of it.

● *Selling a Quality Story*

In an industrial study we conducted for a well-established manufacturer of recycling equipment, we learned how valuable a proven, time-tested reputation can be. When we tested ten selling propositions among buyers of this type of equipment, the winning argument, "Their durability is legendary" outscored the losing one, "On-site training" by nearly 6 to 1 (Buying Index of 180 versus 34). "Made in the U.S.A." scored only in the average range (97 Index).

Recycling Equipment

Question: "When you consider the purchase of industrial recycling equipment, what factor about the company makes it most appealing?"

	Buying Index
Their durability is legendary	180 winner
Made in the U.S.A.	97
On-site training is included	34 loser

Note: An index of 100 is an average response. A total of 400 interviews were conducted nationwide during 1993 among customers and prospects.

This gave the company's sales force new insight into what would persuade buyers to select them over the less expensive foreign imports. As the VP of Sales put it:

You can waste a lot of time selling a weak premise if you don't know in advance what's going to work best. Knowing the "hot buttons" up front enabled our guys to sell hard with the most convincing argument right from the start. Before that, some of our most experienced guys were pushing 'Made in the U.S.A.' when come to find out it wasn't all that important. The 'Legendary durability' story worked much better and in fact our sales team found a whole new selling opportunity based on it: reconditioned equipment. This strategy not only added to our sales revenues, it enabled us to sell more competitively in strictly price situations where a totally reconditioned and guaranteed machine cost much less than a new competitor.

#1, Dominant in Sales or Market

Commanders also like leaders, because they are leaders themselves. If you currently outsell the competition, let them know about it. Here's how Ford did this with an ad for its Escort model. The two-page ad featured a beauty shot of an Escort against a printed background that listed just about every current automobile model known to man. The headline read:

> *If your car is on this list,*
> *Ford Escort outsells it,*
> *Ford Escort. The world's best-selling car.*

My car was on the list. Yours probably was, too.

● *Titleist: The Hitting Power of Being Number One*
Being number one is very important to the action-oriented Commander types. Take Titleist Golf Balls, for example. According to George Sine, Titleist's Director of Marketing Golf Balls—Worldwide:

Being number one is a reinforcement missile which our

sales force promotes to differentiate the brand wherever competitive golf is played.

Our sales force takes every opportunity to reinforce the message that we're number one, including number one in worldwide tour wins and number one with worldwide tour and amateur players, as well as number one in worldwide money winning. We are also quick to reinforce our number one leadership position in product quality, technological innovation, market share, and golfer usage. Being number one is such an integral component of our worldwide sales and marketing strategy that we have successfully registered our "number one" position in conjunction with our name: "Titleist. . .#1 ball in golf." In fact, all of our branding initiatives include this trademark, and every salesperson's salutation references "Titleist, the number one ball in golf."

● *Leadership: A Double-edged Sword*

If you're clearly dominant in the field and everyone knows it, be careful you don't overdo it and make the competition into the perceived *underdog*. This can create a sales backlash and work against you. Here's what Pat Purcell, one of Rupert Murdoch's media troubleshooters in the early '90s, found out in Texas.

In addition to being publisher of the *Boston Herald* at the time, Pat was former sales manager of the *New York Daily News* so he knew what it was like to be on the front lines selling media space. Rupert Murdoch had assigned Pat to take charge of the ongoing San Antonio media battle between Murdoch's *Express News* newspaper and Hearst's *The Light*.

When we conducted sales-based focus group research among current and potential advertisers in both the *Express News* and *The Light*, they claimed that the sales force for the *Express News*, the dominant leader in circulation and sales, had an attitude problem. They appeared to be arrogant and unresponsive, but were unaware of it. Some salespeople were telling advertisers that they shouldn't advertise in *The Light* and that it was going out of business. To further aggravate dual advertisers, the *Express News* sales-people were making it a hassle to share advertising material between papers. As Pat Purcell observed, "Research revealed that this translated to arrogance and made some advertisers less likely to place ad dollars with the *News*. Once we realized this we backed off. This helped the *Express News* significantly increase its share of advertiser dollars and ultimately win the long-standing media battle."

Famous Clients, Famous Founder

Not all amateur photographers are Visualizers by any means. A fair number are Commanders. If they're Commanders, they like to have the best camera equipment—*best* means the camera used by the best photographers. Nikon took advantage of this with an ad that showed an unbroken eleven-year series of Nikon cameras with the year and name of the Pulitzer Prize-winning photographer below each camera, topped by this headline:

> ### The Pulitzer Prize winners may change, but their camera stays the same.
> #### Nikon *We take the world's greatest pictures.*

"Who's using your stuff, anyway?" That's one thing a Commander is always interested in and impressed by. If your client list is impressive, the simplest way to present it is through a detailed client list. However, it's important to point out the most impressive clients in your prospect's kind of business, if possible. The typical Commander will read your client list carefully, looking for any companies with which he is familiar, or any company where one of his friends or business acquaintances is employed. Don't be surprised if he asks you what your company did for a particular client. If you can answer that question, you'll get points, so make sure that you know something about each client on the list.

● *The RIHGA Royal Hotel: Hobnobbing with the Famous*

Telling your prospect about your famous clients works powerfully for Commander types. But if you can get your clients telling *other* prospects about your famous clients, that's even better. The best example of this in our experience involved the RIHGA Royal Hotel in New York. The RIHGA Royal, on 54th Street between Sixth and Seventh Avenues in Manhattan, is right in the middle of the eastern corporate communications and entertainment center of New York. It's surrounded by the headquarters of NBC, CBS, ABC, Time-Warner, SONY, and many others. At fifty-four stories, RIHGA is the tallest pure hotel (no retail or residential space) in New York. Every room is at least a suite. The bathrooms are pink Italian marble with gold-plated fixtures plus separate tub and shower. Its restaurant, The Halcyon, is one of the ten best hotel restaurants in the United States. (Are you impressed yet?) The top twenty-five floors are the Pinnacle Suites, even classier than the lower floors. The rates are tops, too. Frank Banks, the genius hotelier and RIHGA manager who brought the Royal from an anemic 17 percent occupancy rate to a healthy and profitable virtually sold-out status, wanted to push his Pinnacle Suites occupancy rate over the top. He wanted to find out what Pinnacle Suite guests wanted that they didn't already have.

Many RIHGA guests, particularly top-tier Pinnacle guests, are powerful men and women connected in some way to the communications and entertainment business. You can spot the famous entertainers and personalities in the elevators and the lobby: Sting, Diane Sawyer, Terry Bradshaw, Grace Jones, Oliver Stone, and Stevie Wonder. Unless you're in the business, you won't recognize many of the power moguls by name—the sellers of ideas, talent, and money—but they are on the guest registry also. Needless to say, there a more than a few Commanders in this crowd!

So what did these guests want? Our research showed that out of fifteen possible new amenities, guests wanted private telecommunications services: their own private telephone and fax lines; private voice mail; fax machines in the rooms, and cell phones with automatic transfer of incoming calls when they were out of their rooms.

RIHGA Royal Hotel

Question: "What is there about the RIHGA that is most influential in your decision to stay there instead of other hotels?"

Buying Index

Private line, fax machine, and cell phone.................152 winner

Rated "Best Business Hotel" in NY.............................104

Has a 24-hour health club for guests..........................78 loser

Note: An index of 100 is an average response. During 1988 interviews were conducted among a total of 450 guests.

Frank Banks was delighted and had the lines and machines installed. We thought that would be the end of it. But Frank is a Commander himself, and he took it one step further. He arranged for top-tier Pinnacle guests to receive RIHGA business cards in a leather case with their name, private RIHGA telephone number, private cell phone number, and private RIHGA fax number printed right on it (see below)! The cards were an instant hit. Soon, the celebs who roosted at the RIHGA Royal were passing out their new cards to other high-level people. "If you need to get in touch with me while I'm in New York," they would tell them, "here's my number." The card connected the celebrity's name with the name of the hotel as, perhaps, no other form of advertising could.

RIHGA's sales force followed up by promoting the new facilities in the Pinnacle Suites to travel agents who served celebrities and corporate leaders. Ads were also placed in very upscale publica-

RIHGA ROYAL HOTEL
NEW YORK

Nick Philipson

IN RESIDENCE
PINNACLE SUITES
UNTIL May 08, 1998

PRIVATE FACSIMILE: (716) 776-4573
PRIVATE TELEPHONE: (212) 698-3387
PVT CELLULAR PHONE: (917) 307-8752

151 WEST 54TH STREET, NEW YORK, NY 10019
TELEPHONE: (212) 307-5000   FAX: (212) 765-6530

tions, like *CEO*. The calls started coming in. Within four years, the RIHGA was hitting 100 percent occupancy nearly every weeknight.

To stay ahead of the curve, Banks is now introducing video phones in all Pinnacle Suites. Pinnacle guests will be able to see the concierge, or even the general manager. And for frequent Pinnacle guests, Banks will give them a video phone for their homes. What's next, heated toilet seats from Japan? Of course!

● *Northeastern University: Education that Works with Big Name Corporations*

Boston's Northeastern University is huge, with about 20,000 students. It has a number of outstanding schools and courses of study. It also has a very large cooperative education program that connects its students to the world of work. Co-op students spend part of their time in the classroom, and part in occupational settings related to their courses of study. This arrangement is designed to provide NU students with work experience that will make their studies more meaningful and give them a leg up when they enter a job market crowded with other college graduates.

The university wondered which of its features had the greatest appeal among students, staff, graduates, alumni, and prospective students and parents. We tested a number of arguments, strengths, and weaknesses for Northeastern, and found its co-op program to be the most powerful card in its deck.

Northeastern University

Question: "What is there about Northeastern University that makes it most appealing as a place to attend?"

Buying Index

Northeastern's cooperative education program gives
   students experience and a foot in the door....161 winner

Northeastern has 16 convenient campuses in
   the Boston metropolitan area..............................104

Northeastern has good sports teams..........................38 loser

Note: An index of 100 is an average response. During 1986 a total of 1200 interviews were conducted nationally among Northeastern students, staff, graduates, alumni, prospects, parents of students, and parents of prospective students.

The research validated the appeal of that program and led to a refocusing of the university's recruitment efforts, which culminated in an advertising campaign that used the positioning line: "Education That Works." The advertising campaign was supported in sales literature (called recruitment literature in the academic world) and on local billboards. These featured the names of many of the companies that have used Northeastern co-op students, including Gillette, Digital, and Polaroid. In the late '90s, Northeastern is still using this positioning with the added lure of enhanced academic programming, a big rise in the academic preparation of entering students, and much more selective admissions. But endorsements of the co-op program by major U.S. companies remains the key to the success of this campaign.

● *Cambridge Soundworks and Famous Founder Henry Kloss*

Any audiophile who's ever talked to a salesperson at Cambridge Soundworks, the direct distribution speaker company, has probably heard about the company's famous founder, Audio Hall of Fame member, Henry Kloss. The sales force will readily remind you that Henry Kloss was a founder of KLH Speakers (he's the K), plus Advent and Acoustic Research. And if that's not enough, they'll tell you about the outside endorsement the company has received from *Audio* magazine, referring to them as "The Best Value In The World" as you can see in the ad on page 113.

It's no wonder that our client, Cambridge Soundworks, has been such a success on the East Coast and is currently rolling out nationally. In fact, they promote their success in advertising with the claim that they're now the "country's largest factory-direct" speaker company. According to Tom DeVesto, President, "We realize the importance of outside credibility because without our credentials we're just another stereo outlet. When *Audio* magazine says we're special that has ten times more impact than any ad we can create alone."

Winning with Commander Sales Arguments

Commander sales arguments are a great way to introduce yourself, but make sure you are talking to a Commander before you go into any great depth with them.

"The Best Value In The World."

While Commander sales arguments can be used to some effect with most people, Thinkers and Visualizers tire of them quickly. Thinkers may even have a negative reaction. Pay careful attention to the reactions of non-Commanders to these types of sales arguments. They might work against your Thinker or Visualizer prospects if overdone.

Chapter

9

The Thinker Buying Profile: Head Trip Arguments

I think, therefore I am.

RENÉ DESCARTES, 1637

IF YOUR PROSPECT is in the Thinker buying profile and ready to seriously consider your stuff, you need to use selling arguments that have particular appeal to this type of person. Thinker type arguments are combinations of logic, time sequencing, and the *right* way of doing things.

Thinkers like to take their time when considering what is presented to them. Your presentation should be as well organized as possible, so that the facts and arguments build on one another. Be patient and listen carefully to their questions. Thinkers will often dig for detail, so you should be prepared to pull out stuff that other prospects won't bother to ask for. If you're stuck on a question, don't try to fake it or dodge it. Just say "I don't have the answer to that question right now, but I'll get the answer for you." Thinkers would much rather wait for the full answer than work with your half answer. And getting back to the prospect with the answer provides you with an opportunity to engage the prospect once again.

Sales Arguments for Thinkers

Here are five argument categories that are more powerful for Thinkers than for Commanders or Visualizers in the Evaluation step. Ranked in order of effectiveness, they are:

1. Best future results
2. Logical design
3. Best procedures
4. Clever, unique design
5. Endorsed by experts

Best Future Results

Future results are very important to Thinkers. They want to know the consequences of their purchase decisions, and they want you to support your claims with data. The future is the ultimate form of time sequencing, and Thinkers want to know what will happen. Here's how Invesco took advantage of Thinkers' decision processes when new tax legislation created the ROTH IRA— a new type of IRA with a unique set of rules.

> *CONVERT TO A*
> *ROTH IRA AND YOU*
> *MIGHT WIND UP*
> *WITH MORE MONEY.*
>
> *ANY QUESTIONS?*
>
> *WE THOUGHT SO.*
>
> *1-800-220-6792, EXT. 149*
> *INVESCO*
>
> www.invesco.com

Thinkers like to have claims explained and verified. Invesco's 800 number and Web page were designed to provide those details.

● *VHS Videotape: Showing for the Infinite Future*

Sometimes the best way to sell your product is to take the prospect into the future with a unique benefit story. Our work with a major videotape manufacturer back in the early '80s, when the blank videotape category exploded, provides a great example of how this can be done.

When we met with our client's engineers, they were convinced of the superior quality of their product. "Why is your tape better?" we asked. "Our dust-free manufacturing environment," one engineer responded proudly. "It will yield picture perfect quality in the hottest and coldest climate shooting situations," said another. Somehow we couldn't see anyone except people who took family vacations in Lapland or Death Valley getting excited about these qualities—a small market, to be sure. So we kept after the engineers to tell us more about their wonderful tape.

One of the qualities that finally got mentioned was the sheer endurance of the product. It maintained picture quality, no matter how many times it was replayed, or how many times the user taped over previous recordings. To the great surprise of their engineers, consumer research found that nobody cared about dust-free manufacturing, and few people cared about taping quality in extreme temperatures. The most important benefit to potential customers was future, long-term results: original picture quality, no matter how many times the tape was rerecorded or played back. The technical information that the engineers viewed as highly significant mattered little to consumers.

VHS Videotape

Question: "What makes you most interested in buying this brand of videotape?"

Buying Index

Original picture quality no matter how
    many replays...188 winner

Finest sound reproduction..109

Picture perfect in hottest or coldest
    climate conditions...30 loser

Note: An index of 100 is an average response. During 1978, a total of 200 interviews were conducted nationwide among videotape buyers.

Using these findings as support, and with a lifetime guarantee boldly stated on the package, the sales force was able to focus its efforts on an important dimension of quality with great success. What trade buyer could argue with solid consumer research? At that point in time, the blank videotape category was so new that the first company to sit on the long-term quality story owned it. And by the time the competition's sales force realized the importance of future quality, the brand was well entrenched in the category.

● *Outward Bound with New Confidence*

> When you get back, you aren't going to be the person someone thinks you are. You're going to be yourself.
> —FROM THE 1985 OUTWARD BOUND CATALOG

One of our most interesting studies was for Outward Bound. We were asked to help determine the most effective way to position the Outward Bound experience and, more importantly, to generate lead activity for salespeople on a cost efficient basis.

According to Peter Wilhauer, founder of the Hurricane Island school, "What we discovered was that the Outward Bound experience gave graduates enhanced self-confidence that helped them grow as a person. It kept coming back loud and clear from many people who have been through the program."

Outward Bound

Question: "What would you say to recommend Outward Bound to a friend who was considering enrolling in a program?"

Buying Index

You'll grow as a person with new confidence ....187 winner

You'll work as a team and learn new
   interpersonal skills.. 111

There are convenient Outward Bound locations
   all over the country.......................................28 loser

Note: An index of 100 is an average response. A total of 450 interviews were conducted nationwide in 1984 .

The research quantified the "grow as a person" benefit and further indicated that the best way to generate leads was to motivate graduates to bring new people into the program. These graduates were already referring new students. When the organization began rewarding lead generators with free courses, current graduates became even more active in recommending the program. Outward Bound's graduates turned into powerful salespeople and produced referrals at an unprecedented rate.

● *An Eastern Technical School: Jobs Guaranteed for the Future*

Best future results can take the form of benefits that promise a good return on prospects' investments of time and/or money. One eastern technical school client primarily serves male high school graduates who aren't going on to a four-year college. The client learned that it wasn't selling an education or a piece of paper saying "You have graduated." It was selling jobs and future careers that pay *real money.*

The teenage students our interviewers surveyed by telephone were most impressed by the idea that if they graduated from the school they would have an excellent chance of landing a good job with a company that might later help pay for additional education. The new positioning line became "Go There, Grow There," backed by the fact that over 90 percent of the school's graduates actually found jobs in their fields. This argument was so powerful that the school used it effectively for years in everything from one-on-one recruitment to collateral and advertising materials.

Eastern Technical School

Question: "What makes you most interested in going to this school?"

Buying Index

Over 90% of our graduates get a job ....182 winner

We train you in the fastest growing fields..................88

Our program costs are very competitive....................43 loser

Note: An index of 100 is an average response. A total of 450 interviews were conducted among teenage students and prospects during 1986.

Logical Design

Thinkers love a logical design proposition that's ironclad, particularly in language or appearance. Here's how Zip Disks does it.

NOW THAT YOU HAVE A VIRTUAL OFFICE, YOU NEED A VIRTUAL BRIEFCASE TO GO WITH IT.

100MB Zip Disks

● *Progress Software: Selling a Logical Position Worldwide*

Computer people, like programmers, are often (but definitely not always) Thinkers who love logical designs. Progress Software found a selling position that worked especially well with this profile.

At a Progress Software meeting in the '80s, we were sitting around the table with everyone who might have an idea about how to sell Progress Software's new package to management information systems (MIS) people. The company's software allowed users to analyze data from sophisticated existing and new databases. Let's say your company already had a database of current and past business customers with a variety of data about each one, including purchases by product line, date, dollar volume, contact, and so forth. If your company installed the new Progress software, you could use it to zoom in on, for instance, customers in your territory who had previously bought large quantities of the product line your sales manager was pushing with sales force incentives this month. That's the easy part. The hard part, from Progress' point of view, was persuading a company's MIS people to buy this type of software from them instead of from the competition—and there was plenty of competition. What would be the most persuasive argument?

Everyone at the table had an idea. The marketing manager liked "Number one in user satisfaction" and "Market-proven with 40,000 installations." Engineering liked "The power to build critical applications." The salespeople had their own favorite: "Fast application development." The President, Joe Alsop, liked "Productivity with complete control." As two nontechies, who definitely do not speak FORTRAN at home, we leaned toward the simpleminded. We liked "Easy to learn and use." The company's ad agency threw in an unused ad campaign concept: "Gives you complete computing independence."

We prepared to test each of these arguments with a pool of potential customers to find out which had the greater impact and influence. To make things interesting, everyone backed his argument with a $5 bet. The runaway winner out of our pool of arguments was the one offered by the ad agency: a logical "computing independence" selling theme.

Progress Software

Question: "What is the most persuasive aspect of Progress Software when considering a purchase?"

Buying Index

Computing independence: The software is
    portable across all major platforms and
    applications...316 winner

Gives you the power to build critical
    applications...103

Rated number one in the industry by
    outside sources...81 loser

Note: An index of 100 is an average response. A total of 450 interviews were conducted in the United States and Europe during 1989.

The ad agency had, as we mentioned, developed a campaign based on independence six months earlier, but had never run it. A number of visuals were associated with this campaign: the Statue of Liberty, the Berlin Wall coming down, and so forth. Given our research findings, the ad people were now ready and eager to rock and roll with this program—the sooner the better. We urged caution. "Before you run with this campaign," we told them, "let's take a look at what our research respondents really liked about computing independence, and what they related it to." It turned out that when people described what they found appealing in the theme of "computing independence," virtually no one mentioned the word *independence*. Independence just evaporated. What respondents were talking about was platform *portability* and application *portability*, which meant something very specific to MIS people. There was no mental connection between the concept of portability and the notion of independence that was associated with the physical images that our advertising friends were planning to use as the cutting edge of their campaign. Ultimately, the sales force and the ad agency used the new portability selling argument to great effect and Progress Software did very well with it.

Thinkers are generally very precise people, and they use precise language, much more than either Commanders or Visualizers, who are often flamboyant users of language and take lots of liberties with the King's English. So when you are searching for words to represent aspects of your product or its benefits to Thinkers, be careful and rigorous in your choice of words. Use words with the same precision as your prospects.

Best Procedures

Knowing and using the right procedures is important to Thinkers. Using the best procedures over time is more likely to produce better future results, from a Thinker's analysis. Here's the headline from a Noxema Skin Cream ad that illustrates best procedures.

> *THE SECRET TO*
> *BEAUTIFUL SKIN IS*
> *KNOWING HOW TO*
> *WASH YOUR FACE.*
>
> *BEAUTIFUL SKIN BEGINS*
> *WITH NOXEMA.*

● *How Mount Snow Golf School Teed Off on the Competition*

It's surprising how wrong you can be when you base your impressions on hunches and not facts. When we first met with the

folks at Mount Snow Golf School, the leader in its field, it seemed that the best way to sell a golf school was to promote its social aspects, its scenic location, and the fact that a big name pro was associated with the school. However, our research uncovered a totally different motivational cluster. What we learned was that although golf is a physical sport, people who go to golf school aren't there for exercise or even party time. They're there for an education and they want as many logical assurances as possible that their game will improve as a result of the schooling. The number one educational procedure that appeals to these prospects is the *small student ratio*. Their assumption was that if the school followed

the rules and procedures of sound teaching, it would pay off on their score cards.

Here's how the research played out, much to everyone's surprise.

Mount Snow Golf School

Question: "What aspect of Mount Snow's Golf School is most motivating in attending here versus other options?"

Buying Index

Small student/teacher ratio so they can
    take time to build basic fundamentals..............177 winner

Scenic location...89

Big name pros are associated
    with the school...16 loser

Note: An index of 100 is an average response. A total of 450 interviews were conducted nationwide during 1994 among prospects and graduates.

By realizing what prospects really want from a golf school, Mount Snow was able to modify its program accordingly. Its sales force, knowing in advance what prospects wanted, was able to key in on those elements that fit in with the expected procedures of successful teaching—both on the links or in the classroom. According to Peter Johnson, "Refocusing Mount Snow's efforts has led to significant increases in enrollment over previous years. It took the 'I think. You think.' out of the sales process. In fact, 30 percent of our students are return visitors."

Clever, Unique Design

Thinkers focus on design in more than one way. Logical design is a strong motivator, but clever, unique design is another. Thinkers tend to be iconoclasts—they like to break the conventional way of thinking about a product or service. Thinkers will be more receptive to new designs if producers show a fresh approach to the subject. One of the all-time unique designs in the automotive world was the Volkswagen Beetle. Its introductory ad showed a very small picture of a VW "Bug" in a very large ad with very small type that read as follows:

The success of the Bug, one of the weirdest, most unconventionally designed cars to hit the street of North America, is well known. It was especially popular among intellectuals, and Volkswagen has been trying to duplicate its success ever since. In early 1998, it introduced the newly designed Bug. Initial sales pointed to a *sold out* situation for VW's first two years of production (200,000 units). The original Bug's clever, unique design called attention to itself. Then the car's functionality and great gas mileage made Thinkers into believers.

● *Kryptonite: Locking Out the Competition*

Like the VW Bug, Kryptonite Bike Locks has built its success on a blend of design uniqueness and tremendous functionality. It provides an excellent example of how clever, unique design can create attention and buying interest, especially among Thinkers. The Kryptonite lock's U-shape design is such a simple, logical *form follows function* design that a production model has been in the permanent collection of twentieth-century design objects at New York's Museum of Modern Art since 1983. It is, in fact, appealing to just about everyone except bike thieves. Cutting torches, tactical nuclear weapons, and owners' keys are probably the only devices capable of opening a locked Kryptonite.

The Kryptonite design had plenty of logic to it. It turns out that if you are a bicycle thief, your number one tool is a rod cutter. A rod cutter will cut anything round, like a bicycle lock hasp or bicycle chain, for instance. But a rod cutter is useless against a flat band of work-hardened steel, which is exactly what the original Kryptonite bike lock was made of!

The company has done so well with its unique design that it has successfully marketed its family of products in thirty countries. This success has spawned over twenty-five imitations. The design is a winner. So is the name. Kryptonite, if you recall, was that weird material from the planet Krypton that was strong enough to take away Superman's powers. During the early days of the company, founder Michael Zane went to great lengths to emphasize the toughness of his U-Lock design, even going so far as to dress in a Superman outfit and "fly" into buyers' offices.

Endorsed by Experts

Third party endorsements in general can be effective sales tools, but for Thinkers, endorsements by *experts* are more persuasive than endorsements by famous people who aren't experts, like movie stars, or testimonials by the "man in the street." This may be because Thinkers like to think of themselves as experts.

The statement in the following ad for Volkswagen minivans

would be considered blatant puffery had it come from the advertising mill of Volkswagen, but the fact that its source was a prestigious automotive magazine gave it real power among Thinkers.

> ### "The Porsche 911 of vans."
> **Car and Driver**
> ### Nothing else is a Volkswagen

● **Unitarian Universalist Association of Congregations: A Thoughtful Group**

Thinkers are everywhere, but every once in a while we discover an organization that's dominated by Thinkers. Here's how a church discovered through research that endorsements by experts are appealing to both current and potential members.

These days you're selling your service even if you're a religious organization competing with other churches or simply trying to motivate people to get out of bed on Sunday morning. Our research for the Unitarian Universalist Association was funded by a grant and was designed to uncover a unique UUA story that would distinguish this well established religious group.

When we conducted ten focus groups in five representative cities across the country we were all surprised at the impact generated by stories about famous Unitarian or Universalists liberal thinkers. In hindsight, there couldn't be a better way to demonstrate the fact that Unitarians are relevant thinkers than to feature famous intellectual *experts* who were members of the church.

As recapped in the denominational journal, the *UU World*, "The research uncovered the element which makes Unitarian Universalism most appealing to current and potential members; the encouragement of thinking, inquisitiveness and open-mindedness toward one's religion." Knowing this, the UU Historical Society put together thirty pages of backgrounds of famous historical Unitarian public figures in the United States and Canada, including Thomas Jefferson, Susan B. Anthony, Dr. Albert Schweitzer, Louisa May Alcott, Frank Lloyd Wright, Dr. Linus Pauling, and

Clara Barton, Alexander Graham Bell,
Susan B. Anthony, Joseph Priestley

Henry David Thoreau. These were issued to ministers and church members for use in personal contact with potential members, and made available to the public through public relations activities. The program was considered a resounding success. In fact, following the campaign the *Providence Journal* reported, "a Gallup Poll noted a decline in overall churchgoing. The UUA, however, has reversed a decade-long trend of declining membership."

Winning with Thinker Arguments

The key sales arguments described in this chapter will help you engage Thinkers in serious evaluation of your product or service. Your willingness to provide substantiating detail, even if it has to be delivered after the interview, will be much appreciated. Except for the *best future results* argument, which ranks fairly high with all three profiles, the other Thinker arguments are not considered strongly persuasive by Commanders and Visualizers. So, except for future results, make sure your prospects are in the Thinker buying profile when you use the other Thinker sales arguments.

Chapter

10

The Visualizer Buying Profile: Seeing Is Believing

WYSIWYG (What You See Is What You Get)

YOUR PROSPECT IS in the Visualizer Buying Profile, and ready to see your stuff. Visualizers *literally* want to *see* your stuff displayed—in graphic form if possible, with photos, illustrations, charts and graphs, videos, samples, and any other visual forms at your disposal. If you don't have actual samples, pictures, or other graphic representations, paint a picture with words if you can. If you don't know what buying profile your prospect is in, Visualizer sales arguments are often the best ones to start with, as we will show later.

Visualizers like to see a lot of different things in quick succession, so be careful not to bore them with too much detail. And be sure to *show the benefits* of all your sales arguments; they may not have the patience to figure out the benefits on their own.

Sales Arguments for Visualizers

Four argument categories are more powerful for Visualizers than Thinkers or Commanders during the Evaluation step. Ranked in order of effectiveness they are:

1. Clear features = clear benefits
2. Best-looking design
3. Quick and easy
4. Cosmetic appeal

Clear Features = Clear Benefits

Feature = benefit selling is the granddaddy of all sales arguments. It was immortalized in the phrase *Sell the Sizzle, Not the Steak*, coined by the great salesman Elmer Wheeler. Wheeler showed clearly that selling features works best if you immediately sell the associated benefits. A recent headline from an Epson color printer ad adopts this approach directly, as it leads you into specific features and benefits.

> ### WITH ALL THE FEATURES
> ### WE PUT INTO IT,
> ### NO WONDER YOU GET MORE
> ### OUT OF IT.
> ### YOU'VE GOT TO SEE IT
> ### IN EPSON COLOR

For many of us, feature = benefit selling was the *only* way to sell. Our sales training or experience indicated that if we presented each important feature of our product or service, and immediately connected that feature to a specific appealing benefit, we would make the sale. This approach does work; there's no doubt about it. And there are two reasons that it works.

1. Feature = benefit selling works because there are more Visualizers out there than there are Commanders or Thinkers, and Visualizers are moved by this approach.

2. Most people will respond to feature = benefit selling to some degree. If the Visualizer profile is not their preferred buying profile, it's fairly likely to be their secondary profile. In fact, if you can't figure out which profile your prospects are in, we recommend that you begin with Visualizer arguments, feature = benefit arguments in particular. If you observe your prospects closely, you can often get enough cues to determine their preferred profile, and switch to it if necessary.

Although many arguments covered in previous chapters are generic feature = benefit arguments to some degree, the most persuasive types for Visualizers are those that focus on visual or spatial features. Here are three classic cases: industrial, consumer product, and combination.

● The Polaroid EIS Scanner: A Mountain of Detail

A few years ago, Polaroid asked us to evaluate the commercial market for a professional quality industrial graphics scanner that could scan up to 8 x 10-inch photographs and graphic materials. The key was to find out what features and benefits of the scanner would be most appealing and persuasive. The prospects for this unit were professional graphic artists, designers, art directors, and graphic production managers who would use it for commercial printing and prepress graphics preparation. Most of the usage would be for scanning photography of various sorts, from electron microscope photography to long-distance scenic photographs to spacecraft photos of the earth as a big blue dot. You know there was a high percentage of Visualizers in this audience!

The scanner had plenty of features and benefits to test. It could scan an 8 x 10-inch photograph in thirty seconds—six times faster than its fastest competitor at that time. It could also scan up to 256 colors with clear separation; it had 128 levels of gray scale. It scanned up to 600 DPI (dots per inch), and on and on. Polaroid had numerical verification for each of these claims. The big question was, which claim would establish the unit's superiority in the minds of prospective customers?

We interviewed professionals in every category and showed them a series of advertising layouts with actual photographs scanned by the Polaroid unit. The headlines and advertising copy presented the features and numerical specifications of the scanner in detail.

The reactions of our interviewees to Polaroid's numbers were decidedly "underwhelming." Thirty-second scanning was appealing, but only if the quality was superior or at least equal to slower machines. Except for a scattering of technical types, their eyes glazed over at the numbers. Dots per inch, gray scale numbers, color levels, meant little or nothing. They ignored the numbers. "The numbers don't really show us much," they said. What really interested them were the scanned photographs themselves, which they studied very closely. They were particularly attracted to a photograph of a mountain range at twilight. The left side of the mountain was catching the last golden rays of the sun, and the right side was in deep shadow. "That shadow detail is incredible," they all agreed. "If this machine can scan that level of shadow detail in thirty seconds," another said, "I'd buy it in a minute. I don't care what it costs."

So it turned out that shadow detail was the golden yardstick. They needed to see shadow detail in photographs that were particularly difficult to scan and reproduce. Reducing shadow detail to numbers simply would not register with these prospective buyers. They had to *see* it to believe it.

● *Power D-Icer: Freezing Out the Competition with the Right Benefit*

Monson Chemicals had developed a new windshield washer fluid additive that would prevent standard blue water windshield washer fluid from freezing to as low as 25° below zero. "So what's the benefit to users?" we asked. And we guessed that it would have to be good, since the world wasn't exactly waiting for yet another windshield washer fluid to find its way onto the store shelves. In fact, if this product wasn't tangibly different, it wasn't going to get on those crowded shelves at all

The Monson people saw two benefits: "It eliminates the danger of washer fluid freezing up on the windshield while driving," they explained, "and it prevents your washer jets from freezing up."

Having experienced both of these dangerous conditions over the course of many cold New England winters, we thought that these two benefits would plumb the entire universe of possible

benefits for a product of this kind. We were wrong. It turned out that the biggest benefit was one that neither Monson nor we had considered: "Clears ice off your windshield in the morning, from inside your car."

Now, this might not sound like a big deal to people who have garages, but for the great huddled masses who don't, few experiences are as unwelcome as those in which you emerge from your warm kitchen at 7 A.M., briefcase in one hand, mug of hot coffee in the other, and find your windshield encrusted with the previous evening's frozen drizzle. You have ten minutes to beat it down to the commuter rail station, and you have eleven minutes of scraping ahead of you. Choice 1: Take a later train. Choice 2: Pour your hot coffee over the windshield to quickly dislodge the ice—and maybe crack the cold glass.

Monson's new blue water was Choice 3. Yes, this stuff would actually eliminate a thin icy coating from your windshield. All you had to do was hit the windshield sprayer button on your dashboard, run the wipers for a while—maybe giving it another blast of cleaner—and you'd have a clear, clean view of the road. "Beats scraping," we said.

Power D-Icer

Question: "What would convince you to buy Power D'Icer instead of your regular brand of windshield washer solvent?"

Buying Index

Clears ice off your windshield in the morning,
from inside your car .... 196 winner

Removes the danger of frozen washer fluid
on windshields while you're driving 100

Developed by the Colorado School of Mines .... 27 loser

Note: An index of 100 is an average response. A total of 200 prospective buyers were interviewed in the Northeast during 1987.

According to Rom Humphries, consultant to Monson, "When the trade saw the power of the winning benefit, they found room for Power D-Icer, even if it meant kicking a competitive product off the shelf."

● *Fountainhead Technologies: Seeing Clearly in the Swimming Pool*

Fountainhead Technologies had developed Vision, a patented water purification system for swimming pools. This system employed a catalytic technology process that dramatically reduced the amount of chlorine required. But how could they sell this feature? They were looking for the most powerful way to get dealers to switch from recommending conventional systems to recommending Vision, and to reassure customers that the new Vision was a superior product.

We conducted sales research nationally among a combination of consumers (customers and potential buyers), pool supply dealers, and the Fountainhead sales force to find out how consumers and the trade made buying decisions. This research would help us to determine the most powerful selling position for Vision.

Of the ten selling positions we tested, the runaway winner was

"No more chlorine hassles. No odor, red eyes, hair and suit discoloration, or rough, irritated skin." A seemingly powerful claim of "water so clean you can drink it" scored only average, while "patented technology," a claim that the company's scientists thought would win, bombed out.

Vision Water Purification System

Question: "What makes you most interested in using the Vision Water Purification System to clean the water in your swimming pool?"

	Buying Index
No more chlorine hassles	194 winner
Pool water so clean you can drink it	93
Uses a new patented pool filtration technology	15 loser

Note: An index of 100 is an average response. A total of 450 swimming pool owners were interviewed during 1991 in the ten states with the highest incidence of swimming pools.

We knew from the research what would get the trade and consumer's attention, but the research also revealed that the winning claim "no more chlorine hassles" had a believability problem. Though less chlorine use was a benefit, most pool owners weren't exactly staying up nights worrying about the health problems associated with chlorine. As one consumer we interviewed observed, "If chlorine is so bad, why is it added to our drinking water? Sure, I'd probably like to use less chlorine, but I'm not concerned about anyone getting cancer either. And doesn't it take chlorine to kill algae and bacteria and prevent their reoccurrence?"

So we had a strong selling message, but how to give it some bite? Bob Newbert at Duffy & Shanley Advertising, had read through the word-for-word verbatims that consumers associated with the winning "no chlorine hassle" claim and concluded rightly that a promise of overcoming health concerns associated with chlorine should not be the major selling point for the product. Instead, the drawbacks of chlorine had to be tied to a deep, emotional problem which parents could relate to—the fact that children's eyes get burned and red when they swim with their eyes open in a heavily chlorinated pool. A typical consumer response was,

> Chlorine burns your eyes and makes your skin dry out. Chlorine is a real hassle, especially for the kids when they swim underwater with their eyes open. If you can eliminate red eye that's a plus, but it sounds too good to be true. How do I know it'll work? And is this system going to take more work than chlorine?

The dealer research revealed that while they also liked the idea of a pool purification system that required less chlorine, they were concerned that if they recommended Vision to their customers and it didn't perform, they'd have serious problems to deal with.

The challenge was to promote less chlorine use while assuring both dealers and consumers that the product would absolutely work. The product's selling effort was tied to a powerful set of guarantees designed to overcome concerns among dealers and consumers. As a result, the following multipoint guarantee was crucial to the dealers' sales effort, and was also incorporated into all selling materials, packaging, and point of sale materials:

1. Guaranteed safe for children.
2. Guaranteed to use less chlorine.
3. Guaranteed to require less pool maintenance.
4. Guaranteed easy to use.
5. Guaranteed to work.

In addition, the advertising agency brought the "safe for children" claim to life by developing a powerful icon for the Vision brand: a smiling young girl swimming underwater with her eyes open among brightly colored tropical fish. The rationale was as follows:

> Young girl = Safe for kids
> Open eyes = No burning
> Smiling = Enjoyable swimming experience
> Fish = So natural it's safe enough for fish

Newbert observed,

For water purity
you can see and feel.
And it installs
in just minutes.

The **Nature²** Natural Pool Purifier
for Cartridge Filters

"Fishgirl" as we call her, immediately communicated all the key attributes for the product: it's safe, natural, and enjoyable. She also made a technology product more approachable in much the same way an Apple made a high-tech product (personal computers) more user friendly for the mass market. One picture truly was worth a thousand words. The sales force used Fishgirl in every sales pre-

sentation to dealers, all sales brochures, all advertising, and on every package. She became our Pillsbury Doughboy and was soon universally identified with Vision within the industry.

The Fishgirl approach succeeded beautifully because it took a basic technological feature "less chlorine," and delivered it with a cluster of benefits "safe for kids, no burning eyes, natural, and enjoyable," that were communicated simultaneously through one very strong visual demonstration.

Best-looking Design

Every once in a while we see a product that is just so pleasing to the eye or to the touch that little else must be said to capture our attention and appreciation: a Saab 900 convertible, a Mont Blanc fountain pen, a Louis silk tie, or a Kohler sink faucet. Yes, a sink faucet! Each of these products achieves a seamless integration of form and function that sets it apart from its competitors. The design is so artfully rendered that the product speaks for itself.

The Kohler high-fashion household faucets and plumbing fixtures ads have brilliantly captured the entire visual design approach in five little words.

> ## THE BOLD LOOK OF KOHLER

If you're lucky enough to represent a product that has a *best-looking design*, show it off! It's your best selling tool, especially for Visualizers, for whom best design arguments are very compelling.

● *A Compact Stereo System for the Rest of Us: The Walls Are the Enemy*
Visualizers respond to three-dimensional shape as well as two-dimensional pictures. In a major stereo brand study, we ran into a classic case of three-dimensional Visualizer sensitivity.

Up to that time, the company had been very successful in designing and selling high-end stereo equipment including the speaker systems. They wanted to introduce a superior compact sound system featuring its speakers at an affordable price. In 1990 they asked us to research a compact music system designed for the general public. The unit we tested was a three-piece unit with a central receiver and two separate speakers. The big question was, how could the company sell this sophisticated yet inexpensive system to the general public? The audiophile knew the company and what it represented. The "man on the street" did not. There were many three-piece units on the market already, most of mid- to low-quality. How could our client get the public—few of whom were sound connoisseurs—to respond to this quality product?

For the engineers, the answer was simple. "Sell it on the basis of our superior electronic technology," they told us. They were referring to the sophisticated design system that had made them famous. The marketing and advertising people weren't so sure. They understood what the engineers did not: outside a small circle of sound buffs, few, at that time, had ever heard of the company. Working with the company, we developed ten different selling arguments for testing. One was that their special electronic technology produced sound with "concert hall realism." That's what the unit really did, and that's what had made the company famous with audiophiles, who, if you stereotype them, were your logic-oriented types. The sort of people who drive a ten-year old Volvo and keep a copy of *Stereo Review* on their nightstand.

So how should this product be communicated to consumers? We tested ten different benefits and discovered that "shapes the sound to fit the shape your living room" was more appealing than all others, including "concert hall realism."

New Compact Stereo System

Question: "What is there about the system you just heard that makes you most interested in buying one for your home?"

Buying Index

Adjustable vanes in the speakers tune the system to the shape of your living room 191	winner
True "big speaker sound" in a small system............102	
Delivers fine quality component sound 52	loser

Note: An index of 100 is an average response. A total of 300 consumers were interviewed in New England in 1990.

In the demonstration rooms where we did the interviewing, we had people drawing pictures of the shape of their living rooms, dens, and bedrooms to show us how they would position the speakers to fill the space! They were clearly in the Visualizer profile when describing how the speakers would work in their homes. For them, the three-dimensional room configuration and the furniture that blocked or absorbed sound were the enemy, and this new system could help overcome this three-dimensional problem.

Quick and Easy

We mentioned earlier that Visualizers like a quick pace in a sales presentation. Actually, they like a quick pace in anything, and quick and easy go together in a Visualizer's frame of reference. Here's a great product ad for Visualizers:

> *REVOLUTIONARY NEW KIND OF*
> *DRAIN OPENER INVENTED;*
> *UNCLOGS DRAINS IN 1 SECOND*
>
> *AMAZING NEW*
> **DRAIN POWER**

Visualizers gravitate towards anything that is simple to use, fast, or—even better—*instant*. Thinkers believe that *"anything worth having is worth waiting for,"* but Visualizers *want it now!* They want automobiles they can drive off the lot. (Why else would auto dealers maintain huge on-site inventories?) They want furniture that they can take home when they buy it. They want faster computers and, since they cannot stand the "World Wide Wait," they want the fastest modems on the market.

● *Polaroid's Instant 35mm Success*
We mentioned earlier a study we did for Polaroid on behalf of a new scanner. Another study for Polaroid's Commercial Imaging Group was for its Color Film Recorder, a computer peripheral that

turns PC or Mac graphics into stunning 35mm color slides or overheads for presentations. Telephone research among current and potential customers, primarily in medicine, science, education, and training markets, proved that speed and convenience are the key factors among these Visualizers. When asked to rate various appeals of Polaroid's Color Film Recorder, "speed-oriented" benefits ran away with it, outscoring both "quality" and "productivity." Not that quality and productivity weren't important, but they were less likely to motivate purchase interest than speed, because time is money.

Polaroid Color Film Recorder

Question: "What would motivate you to purchase this product?"

	Buying Index
Faster than sending materials out	159 winner
Professional-level quality	104
Increased productivity	62 loser

Note: An index of 100 is an average response. A total of 250 corporate decision makers were interviewed nationally during 1992.

According to Bob Boucher, Marketing Communications Director for the Polaroid Commercial Imaging Group, "Once we realized how important speed and ease of use were for this product, we were able to deliver a story that had immediate acceptance because it fit the potential buyer's priorities."

● *Liberating 400,000 Mac Mice*
Back in the '80s, one of the our first high-tech clients realized the value of *quick and easy* in their sales arguments for introducing the new hard drive for Macintosh computers. Research revealed the importance of speed as a feature, and the cutting of waiting time as the key benefit of speed, for both the trade and the consumer markets.

Computer Hard Drive for Macintosh

Question: "How would you justify buying this new product?"

Buying Index

Cuts waiting time ....174 winner

Allows you to run sophisticated software.................103

Doesn't take up valuable desk space...........................58 loser

Note: An index of 100 is an average response. A total of 200 corporate decision makers were interviewed nationwide during 1979.

The company's sales literature featured the headline, "Announcing the Liberation of 400,000 Mice." The body copy stated that "This message is for the people who bought Macintosh because of its user-friendliness—and then found it a bit slow in expressing its affections." Today, nearly twenty years later, speed is still the name of this game.

Cosmetic Appeal

How do you sell cosmetic appeal in words? That was the challenge for Clairol, and the resulting campaign worked so well that it is has become an all-time advertising classic.

> *Does she. . .or doesn't she?*
>
> **Hair color so natural only her hairdresser knows for sure!**
>
> *Miss Clairol*

● *MediSense: It Looks Just Right*

Selling strong cosmetic appeal can put you ahead of the competition, especially among the Visualizers, and especially if you can prove it with facts and figures. Here's an example of cosmetic appeal for a credit-card size medical device that measures blood glucose levels for diabetes patients.

Our work with MediSense in testing a variety of new blood

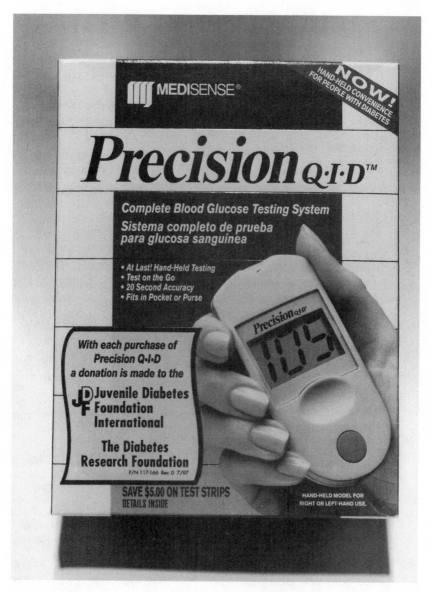

glucose monitor designs uncovered a winner. The key was keeping the readout numbers as large as possible while reducing the size of the rest of the meter to make it as inconspicuous as possible—because the majority of users do not want to draw attention to the fact that they are testing their blood. The new, smaller, streamlined Model A significantly outscored the larger-sized market leader as well as two other MediSense prototypes.

This visual difference, coupled with the research which showed that consumers preferred the MediSense PRECISION QID size, were used very effectively by the sales force to sell the product successfully to the trade. And when it was introduced to the public, it was such a popular model that it exceeded company sales projections. The MediSense Model A outscored the prototype Model C by more than two to one. Without testing, the company might have missed a major opportunity.

In 1996 the company was purchased by Abbott Labs, which paid $45 for each share of MediSense Inc., making winners out of any investors who bought the stock for $12 two years earlier.

Winning with Visualizer Arguments

Feature = benefit selling will work fairly well with most prospects, but it works best with Visualizers. The secret of selling feature = benefit stories to Visualizers is to sell a lot of them quickly, and make sure you don't miss any benefits. Quick and easy sales arguments are a fast and simple way to grab a Visualizer's attention. And great looking designs, as well as cosmetic appeal can sell themselves if you present them in a visually dramatic way.

In the next chapter, we'll up the ante. We'll show you how to handle situations in which you need to sell to more than one buying profile at a time.

Chapter

11

Handling Three Profiles at Once

All together now. Ah-one, Ah-two, Ah-three.

<small>Lawrence Welk</small>

Stay On Your Prospects' Buying Path

There are three situations in which you may need to use more than one style of language and argument to make a sale. Two of these situations are a function of presenting to several people with different buying profiles at the same time, either in large noninteractive groups or smaller interactive groups. The third situation arises when you are talking one-on-one with a single prospect, but the prospect changes buying profiles one or more times during the conversation.

Situation 1: Here, you're selling to a large group in a primarily noninteractive presentation, typically with slides, overheads, or other visual support. When more than about eight or nine people are in the audience, there is a very high likelihood that some will be in the Commander profile, some in the Thinker profile, and some in the Visualizer profile. And usually you don't know the leader of the group well enough to know what her dominant personal buying profile is.

Situation 2: In this case, you're selling interactively to a small group such as a product team that has members who may fall into different profiles, and who ask different kinds of questions. In this situation you are more likely to know the leader's dominant buying profile, but unlikely to know the buying profiles of the other group members beforehand. You may never know the profiles of the group members who speak little or not at all during your presentation.

Situation 3: In the third situation, prospects you are working with one-on-one may change from their initial buying profile to another profile or profiles in the middle of the interview. For instance, in the Evaluation step they may switch from their initial Commander profile to the Thinker profile and finally to the Visualizer profile as you progress from answering questions about your company's background and market dominance to your prospect's detailed questions on your product design, and finally its special features and benefits.

In each of these situations, there are techniques that will help you cover and stay on your prospects' buying path from start to finish

The 1-2-3 Approach to Effective Large Group Presentations

When presenting to a large audience likely to contain prospects in various buying profiles, the most effective way to insure that as many prospects as possible are persuaded by your message is to follow the rhetorical format originally developed by the Greeks for philosophical, political, and legal argumentation: present your message in three parts.

Part 1: Use Commander arguments that create and enhance your credibility, your background, the longevity of your company, and its dominance or leadership in the business. This will give the audience reasons to believe what you have to say.

Part 2: Offer Thinker arguments that establish the logic and common sense associated with your product or service. This will give listeners a basis for understanding what your product is all about, and reassure them that your approach has been carefully thought out.

Part 3: Use Visualizer arguments that create visual images of your product's most important features and communicate the emotional power of the benefits of those features.

End your formal presentation by summarizing what you've just said and accentuate the overall emotional benefits of your offer.

This three-part format presents specific arguments that are, in turn, especially persuasive to Commanders, Thinkers, and Visualizers. It insures that no one is left feeling that you failed to address the issues important to them. Language is a critical element of this technique. It works best if you *deliver each part in the same language profile as the arguments!* So when you are delivering the Commander background arguments, you'll be using Commander language, emphasizing the *weight* of your experience, the *power* of your market leadership, and the enthusiasm your company personnel *feel* for the product or service. When you deliver your Thinker arguments, you'll use Thinker language to emphasize how much *thought* went into the design of the product. Describe how it represents a breakthrough in *understanding* and *thinking* about the product category. When you present the Visualizer arguments, you'll use Visualizer language to show them the big *picture* and *illustrate* each feature *graphically*. Give examples of the *emotional* benefits associated with each.

One of our larger group presentations was made for a major defense manufacturer. One of the divisions of the company makes "black boxes." We never found out what the black boxes were, but we were told that a substantial proportion of the mobile equipment used by the United States in the Gulf War had one of their black boxes in it.

The new company CEO wanted to improve the company's relations with suppliers, so they could communicate more efficiently, prepare bids faster and with lower prices, and perform their work more efficiently, with fewer surprises. This in turn would allow them to be more efficient and more competitive in bidding on major government contracts.

We interviewed a large random sample of the company's suppliers to obtain opinions on how communications with them could be improved. Once our interviewing was completed, we were asked to present our findings to an assembly of their network of suppliers. This was an unusual project for us because we typically interview sales prospects, rather than vendors. But the project presented two important opportunities for us: 1) a chance to help the U.S. defense effort and gain a prestigious client, and 2) an opportunity to personally present the results of our research in a huge convention hall full of top managers representing over six hundred companies—everything from metal benders, to optical specialists, to sophisticated software firms.

The big question was, how do you present research in a way that makes it compelling to everyone in the hall? We assumed that this audience would contain a typical distribution of Commanders, Thinkers, and Visualizers. Following the classic Greek rhetorical model, we started the presentation with our company background including our twenty-plus years in opinion research; a list of important clients like IBM, Polaroid, General Motors, and Harvard University; and our key PhD. personnel. Next we described the logical design of the interviewing approach, along with its analytical tools. Then we illustrated the results and recommendations, including the emotional benefits of being able to quickly and easily see the right people at the various supplier corporations, to gain a clear picture of what they company really wanted, and to do business with them over the long haul in a profitable and mutually beneficial manner.

The response was genuinely enthusiastic. You'll be able to generate the same kind of enthusiasm in large group presentations if you follow the same three-part approach, addressing the interests of all three buying profiles in their corresponding languages.

Small Group Presentations

Extensive research at Tufts University's Fletcher School of Law and Diplomacy has shown that small decision-making work groups typically take on the decision-making characteristics of the group leader or leaders. A work group almost always has a "process" leader, usually the official leader of the group, who mediates the discussion and leads the group towards a consensus. A work group also often has a "task" leader, another person who is more concerned with getting the "right" answers than generating a comfortable consensus.

When you make a presentation to a small group, then, it is useful to know who the official leader is, and identify the real process leader and the real task leader. Other individuals may have influence as well. In many cases, you will not have the opportunity to determine in advance "who's who" and which buying profiles are involved. So, how do you work with such a group?

Because groups typically take on the buying profiles of their leader(s), your first task is to figure out who the process and task leaders are and what their buying profiles are. The best way to manage this is to give a very brief overview of your organization and then ask for an open discussion. For instance, an earlier chapter referred to our technique of tossing a report on the table, upside down, and saying: "If this were our final report for you, what critical issues would you want it to answer?" In this scenario, in the discussion that follows, *they* do the talking and you do the listening. In most cases, they will tell you what they need and want to buy. The process and task leaders will reveal themselves along with their buying profiles. The biggest challenge is to remain quiet while keeping your eyes and ears open and receptive to important cues.

Once you've learned the lay of the land, you can begin addressing the group's needs with sales arguments. In most cases, you should select sales arguments that will have the strongest appeal *to the process leader's buying profile, being sure to use the leader's own language*. But the task leader is also important, so fill in with the task leader's buying profile arguments and language when you can. When questions or objections come up, strive to answer them in the buying profile and language suggested by the questions or objections themselves.

In the wrap-up, return to the original needs outlined in the "final report" and reinforce your proposed solution with sales arguments in the leader(s) buying profiles.

This approach is very different from a "canned" approach, and requires more concentration and flexibility on your part. The rewards, however, will be immediately obvious to you. You'll get a level of positive response and enthusiasm that you never received from small group presentations before, and you'll gain the satisfaction of knowing you've presented and they've understood the best that you have to offer.

● *Institutional Retirement Plan: Dual-Profile Selling*

One of our most interesting financial studies was done on behalf of a major mutual fund's Institutional Retirement Plan, which was marketed to large corporations. This experience demonstrates the importance of being flexible and selling to the modality of the prospect.

In the mid-'90s we conducted a number of in-depth one-on-one interviews nationally among treasurers, human resource managers, and benefits managers at major corporations in Boston, Chicago, New York, and Dallas. The research was conducted off-site at focus group facilities with one-way mirrors for client viewing. Respondents received a $150 cash incentive for twenty minutes of their time. To maximize cooperation and interest, the company was identified as the study's sponsor. The purpose of the research was to determine the buying path used by these three kinds of executive decision makers in selecting an Institutional Retirement Plan.

These people were very concerned both with retirement plans and how vendors could help educate employees about the plans and investment choices. It seems that the government required businesses to educate employees who had funds in 401(k) plans. However, the government failed to spell out the criteria for fulfilling that requirement. It hadn't told businesses how it intended to evaluate their employee 401(k) education programs. It was as if the government said, "Hey you've got to pass the test, but we're not going to tell you what you're being tested on." This ambiguity left everybody in a state of anxiety, and many looked to vendors to help provide employee education.

We soon learned that the three groups of business prospects we interviewed operated in two primary profiles, depending on title. The treasurers/CFOs were the Thinkers. They wanted logical explanations presented in crisp detail. They were interested in bottom-line performance more than the impact on employee morale. They approached the decision from an intellectual perspective. Education appealed to them, but only if it was presented in a logical, programmed way.

As they looked through the sample brochures, these Thinkers zeroed in on detailed copy that described, step by step, what the company would do to help firms educate their employees. They also reacted uniformly to various sample brochure covers our client wanted tested. To a person, the logical financial types disliked covers that had a fuzzy background.

The human resource managers and benefit managers approached these same issues very differently from the treasurers/CFOs. They were primarily Commander types who had "people issues" on their minds. They were concerned about how different companies, like our client, could help employees to use their 401(k) plan, become more involved in the process, and eventually have more confidence in their ability to make investment choices. This group liked pictures of people because they were people oriented. They adopted an empathic, sympathetic approach to our client's concern for employee education. They had an inner sense of how an employee-participant could be confused by the investment process, and they believed on a "gut" level that the ideal plan would be people oriented.

As a result of this research, the sales materials prepared to support the Institutional Retirement Plan were created for both Thinkers and Commanders. They contained crisply presented logical arguments, but there were also people's photos with feel-oriented arguments and words. According to the manager on the project, "We realized that it was a dual sell to different kinds of decision makers. I think we saved a lot of time and energy by doing some homework up front, finding what made these people 'tick' and how we could present our services in the most compelling manner."

One-on-One Buying Profile Changes

Some prospects stay in their initial buying profile throughout a one-on-one presentation. Nevertheless, they may be interested in sales arguments from buying profiles that are not their dominant profile. So if you have particular sales arguments that you know to be very powerful, but not in the prospect's dominant profile, use them. Other prospects change profile in the course of a presentation. Some, like experienced purchasing agents, methodically check out your sales arguments in all three buying profiles, one at a time, starting with the buying profile most important to them and ending with the least. Still others have two profiles they use with almost equal frequency. Some ask key questions that don't correspond with their dominant buying profile. They ask these because experience has taught them that they must if they hope to avoid buying mistakes—for example, the car buyer who is a dyed-in-the-wool Visualizer, but who knows that she must get into the mechanical specs of the vehicle if she hopes to find a car with high performance ratings. The more experience prospects have with purchase decisions, the more likely they will be interested in more than one set of profile-associated sales arguments. Just remember to stay with their dominant buying profile language, regardless of the sales argument category. Of course, if you detect that prospects have changed *their* profile language, you must also change yours.

➡ **The Commander.** If you are talking about your client list (a Commander sales argument) to a prospect in the Commander profile, your job is easy. You might say, "Our client list includes some of the largest and most prestigious clients in your field, including XYZ Company, the market share leader. I'm sure you know some of the executives we deal with, and I'd be happy to provide you with client names and phone numbers for referrals."

➡ **The Thinker.** If you are talking about your client list to a prospect in the Thinker buying profile, you might say, "Here is our detailed client list that covers every major category of installation. The logic of our product design philosophy provides the flexibility to meet critical specifications and requirements in virtually every important application in your field. Here's how some of these design and engineering applications work."

◆ **The Visualizer.** If you are talking about your client list to a prospect in the Visualizer buying profile, you might say, "As you scan through our client list, you'll see clients from many different companies in your field. Our products are used in a wide variety of ways that you may not have seen before. Let me show you some interesting pictures of these unusual applications, which may look quite different from what you usually see."

It's like patting your head and rubbing your tummy at the same time. It seems really difficult, but it gets easier more quickly than you would expect. It helps enormously if you prepare your major sales arguments, such as your client list, in all three language profiles in advance. That way, you won't have to make them up on the spot.

Only rarely will you come across prospects who change profiles completely, including the language. Again, the rule of thumb says: *Don't change your language profile unless the prospect changes her language first.*

When to Take Your Best Shots

What do you do when you know that the key evaluation arguments that differentiate you from your competition are not in your prospect's dominant buying profile? Timing and language are the solutions to this situation. Start with one or two evaluation arguments in the *prospect's* dominant buying profile, even though you know that in general these arguments are not your strongest differentiators. You may be surprised at the positive reaction you receive from these arguments. They show prospects that you are on their wavelength, and that you understand how they make decisions. Having established that, you are ready to present key arguments from the most effective buying profiles. For maximum impact, present them in the prospect's dominant *language* profile, as we illustrated before. The combination of timing and right language gives you the opportunity to use all of your evaluation arguments in the most persuasive way.

Reaching Beyond Your Own Profile

● *Selling the Sizzle, the Lobster, and the View*

One of our favorite clients is Anthony Athanas, founder of Anthony's Pier 4 restaurant in Boston, perhaps the most famous seafood restaurant in the world. At the young age of 87 when we worked with him, Anthony was still working seven days a week, ten hours a day!

The year Anthony opened his first restaurant, Anthony's Grill, in Lynn, Massachusetts back in 1937, he attended the national restaurant show in Chicago where he heard the famous salesman, Elmer Wheeler, speak about *Selling the Sizzle, Not the Steak*. Anthony listened carefully. He recalls, "It was the hottest summer I could remember and I was getting killed by the two biggest restaurants in town, Hunt's Grill and Basil's. They were jammed with customers, while my place was dying on the vine, primarily be-

cause they had their big Carrier and York air conditioners." Anthony knew he needed air conditioning to be competitive, but he needed a selling point too. Then he got an idea. Lynn was the hometown of General Electric. In fact the company supported thousands of Lynn families. Anthony remembers,

> My mission was to find a GE air conditioner somewhere, anywhere. It took me quite a while to find one. I had to order it from Ft. Wayne, Indiana, but I got the only air conditioner in Massachusetts with the General Electric name. I talked it up with my customers and started running ads in the local newspaper. Before I knew it, the GE people were streaming into my restaurant, including the manager of the plant, Nick Dushman (who I later named a sandwich after). Soon, Anthony's Grill was on the map, with famous customers ranging from Ronald Reagan (spokesman for GE at the time) to presidential candidate Harry Truman, who dropped in for a cup of coffee (the year the newspapers printed the wrong headline, "Dewey Beats Truman").

Anthony is a natural Commander. He loves people and is proud of the famous guests that have visited his restaurant. Their pictures are everywhere to be seen. Famous guests over the years include Jesse Owens, Bobby Orr, John F. Kennedy, Julia Child, Arthur Fiedler, Rocky Marciano, Frank Sinatra, Willie Mays, Elizabeth Taylor, and Joe DiMaggio to name just a few.

Anthony has always known the importance of offering the highest quality food, but over time he also acquired a keen sense of, as he put it, "packaging it with a blue ribbon." Over the years Anthony learned how to sell people on his restaurants using all three selling profiles.

Research uncovered a winning new three-prong advertising campaign in story form by Anthony himself, directed to Commanders ("Years in business with famous clients"), Thinkers ("Their own fleet of lobster boats in Maine to assure the finest quality for now and the future") and Visualizers ("The best view in Boston"). Anthony uses them all, and has a knack for using the right story for the right person.

Anthony's Pier 4 Restaurant

Question: "What makes you most interested in dining at Anthony's Pier 4 restaurant?"

Buying Index

Their own dedicated fleet of Maine
    lobster boats ....166 winner

In business serving famous clients
    since 1937..154 winner

Best view in Boston..137 winner

A real person and his family are behind
    the business...108

One of Boston's few restaurants
    with free parking..67 loser

Note: An index of 100 is an average response. A total of 300 interviews were conducted among current and prospective customers during 1997.

Selling Everybody, All the Time

As you gain expertise in handling these situations, your ability to generate real enthusiasm for your products and services will increase dramatically. It's a wonderful feeling to know you are maximizing your sales power with any kind of prospect, not just the ones that are like yourself.

Chapter

Step 4: Where to ACCESS the Product

It ain't over till it's over.

Yogi Berra, 1973

Will They Buy the Product You Just Sold, From You?

If you are a distributor, wholesaler, retailer, or reseller of any kind, the last thing you want to do is convince your prospects to buy a product or service that you represent, only to have them *access*, or purchase, it from someone else! That's winning the battle but losing the war. This is a particularly serious danger when the decision will be made at a later date—when you're not around to take the order, which is often the case. To insure against this possibility, you must make convincing arguments that *your* company is the best one to provide the product or service. If your arguments are strong enough, you can get the order without the prospect even bothering to seriously check out other suppliers. And if you are the sole source of the product, these arguments will increase your chances of closing the sale.

Having decided to buy the product or service you offer, your prospects are now at the point of wanting to reduce the risk of the purchase as much as possible. Even if they do not ask for reassurances, you must provide them at this buying step. The more assurances they have that dealing with you and your company will be risk-free, the less likely they will be to drift to alternate sources, delay the decision, ask for competitive bids, or reverse the purchase decision.

The four most powerful argument categories to assure that the product or service is ordered from you instead of another reseller, ranked in order of effectiveness, are:

1. Enhanced guarantees
2. Delivery on demand
3. Fix any problem, overcome all obstacles
4. Personal attention

Enhanced Guarantees

The product or service you're selling may have its own guarantees and warranties. *This takes care of the product risk, but not the vendor risk.* The most powerful way to insure that your prospects don't buy somewhere else is to reduce the perceived risk of buying from *you*. You can accomplish this by selling the additional, enhanced guarantees or warranties of your own company, either written or unwritten. Enhanced guarantees are guarantees that you, the reseller, *add on top of* whatever guarantees or warranties the original product or service carry.

The only time we've seen the opposite approach work was in an unusual ad written for Myron the Greek by the great copywriter Ray Welch:

> ## Our Iron-Clad Guarantee:
> ## You bought it, You own it.
>
> *Myron the Greek's Jeans Store, Boston*

● *Tech Hifi: 10 Reasons to Buy Here*

Your company may already have explicit enhanced guarantees. One of the best we've ever seen was from Tech Hifi, an early leader in high fidelity equipment.

Tech Hifi was one of our first clients back in the late '70s. It was a retail operation selling stereo gear in New England. The chain was riding the crest of the stereo boom at the time, but began feeling the pressure of competitive entries. Dropping the price was one way to differentiate the chain, but that would be disastrous to the bottom line. Instead, Tech Hifi used sales-based research to uncover a potent new sales strategy that differentiated them from the competition and gave their sales force something powerful to talk about: The 10-Point Buyer Protection Plan.

The Tech Hifi Buyer Protection Plan

1. Satisfaction guaranteed, or your money back. (7-day 100% refund)
2. 90-day 100% trade-in allowance
3. One-year speaker trial
4. 60-day defective exchange (new unit if not repaired in 5 days)
5. 30-day price protection
6. 1 to 5 year labor guarantee (5 years on speakers, 3 on electronics, 1 on decks and players)
7. Free setup of critical items
8. Free consultation services
9. Free in-store testing
10. Free overseas conversion

Here's how the guarantees ranked in the research versus other sales arguments.

Tech Hifi

Question: "What is there about Tech Hifi that influences you most to buy here versus the competition?

Buying Index

10-Point buyer protection plan ....192 winner

Widest selection of components................................106

Rated #1 in independent surveys................................49 loser

Note: An index of 100 is an average response. A total of 250 interviews were conducted in Boston during 1979 among a combination of current customers and prospects.

Actually, the guarantees had been in place for over a year, but weren't being used by the salespeople because they were concerned they might lose commissions if customers started bringing back the equipment. The research gave management the ammunition it needed to convince the salespeople that guarantees were an opportunity, not an obstacle. According to Rick Deutsch, Director of Marketing, "This finally convinced the salespeople to talk about the guarantees. Until then they viewed guarantees on the downside. They thought customers would be back and 'there goes my commission.' When they saw the numbers they realized that they had a real opportunity to overcome consumer hesitation by offering people the chance to change their minds. In fact, less than 1 percent of the equipment ever came back. Our sales jumped over 40 percent in less than a year from actively promoting the guarantees."

Your company may offer a number of enhanced guarantees as common business practice, but they may not be written down anywhere. Find out what they are and get permission to use them whenever you need them. You'll find that these guarantees are one of the most powerful ways to insure that you don't lose the sale.

Delivery On Demand

When prospects ask you about delivery, you know it's a buying signal. How you answer the question can make or break the sale. Ideally, you want to be able to deliver on demand, and with certainty. We all know how FedEx says it.

> ## *If it absolutely, positively has to be there overnight.*
> ### *FedEx*

Sometimes guaranteed delivery time is so important that you can eliminate the competition altogether by promising on-time delivery, especially if you back it up with a guarantee, as FedEx has done. If the FedEx package doesn't arrive on time, the delivery is free! In fact, if you call FedEx to find out where your package is, they can give you its current location anywhere on the planet! And when your client calls to complain that the package never arrived, you can put him on hold, call FedEx, and get the name of the person who signed for it at the client's office. What fun it is to casually show the client how buttoned up you are when you tell him that his assistant, John Doe signed for it at 9:34 A.M. FedEx considers guaranteed delivery so important for keeping the competitive edge that it prints the registered statement "The World On Time" on every FedEx package. Have you ever tried to call the post office to find out exactly where your guaranteed overnight package is? That's just a waste of time!

The *method* of delivery is sometimes as important as the *date* of delivery. L. L. Bean can deliver its clothing and gear quickly using the U.S. Postal Service, UPS, or FedEx. However, during the holiday gift-giving season, they make a big deal of shipping through FedEx. FedEx's strong image of offering "on-time delivery" is more important than being cheaper. When you're buying a gift for Christmas you don't want to take the chance that it will arrive on December 26th! FedEx also has a more upscale image than its competitors, and L. L. Bean benefits from that image.

● *Charles River Laboratories: Live Delivery—Any Way You Want It*
Charles River Laboratories, a leading worldwide provider of laboratory animals, stresses the importance of delivery methods,

and gauges their performance regularly through customer satisfaction surveys. As Gil Slater, VP of Customer Relations put it,

> Since live product is being transported, delivery is very important to our clients, but we discovered that in our business the method of delivery is actually more important than the date of delivery. We had traditionally used a combination of company-owned trucks supplemented by outside air freight. Customers expressed their very strong preference for delivery in our own vehicles. They were apparently concerned about the possible stress which test animals might go through at high altitudes where they thought lower temperatures could reduce resistance to disease. We responded by extending truck routes into new areas. Concurrently, our sales force promoted this as a specific benefit to current and potential customers. . .one which would assure quality control. It not only improved our satisfaction scores among customers, it attracted new ones and generated an increase in business. By continuing the survey process annually, we can determine the hierarchical listing of features and benefits. So we really know what is important to our customers and can focus on selling and providing what they really want, not what we think they want.

Fix Any Problem, Overcome All Obstacles

Potential problems, including those that are not directly related to the performance the product, are another risk to the buyer. A reseller's expertise in overcoming problems and a willingness to share that expertise provide strong motivation to buy from that reseller, even if price and delivery methods are not the best available. RadioShack runs an ad campaign that sells this argument.

> *You've got questions.*
> *We've got answers.*
> *RadioShack*

Sometimes you need to sell prospects on the fact that your company can fix virtually any problem.

● *One Man to One Machine*

Our work with one of the largest distributors of copiers in the United States in the late '80s demonstrates the importance of selling your product based on long-term solutions to problems, not just today's immediate purchasing criteria. When we asked office managers about their greatest concern with regard to purchasing copier equipment, they described three factors, and weighted them equally: price (28 percent), quality (27 percent) and maintenance service (27 percent). However, when we tested sales arguments for purchasing copiers from a particular distributor, the risk of getting bad service rose to the top, and a technical service sales argument beat out nine others.

Business Equipment Dealer

Question: "Much of this equipment can be purchased else-where. What motivates you most to buy from us?"

Buying Index

You can count on our service support ....240 winner

Provides best overall value 110

In business for over 25 years..30 loser

Note: An index of 100 is an average response. A total of 300 interviews were conducted in the Northeast among office managers at current and prospective firms.

The research showed clearly that the office manager's biggest nightmare is the broken copier because every time it is "down" a different technician shows up, starts from scratch, and hopefully fixes the machine. Then when it goes down again, the cycle starts all over. That's when no one remembers how much the office manager saved when the copier was purchased.

The distributor solved this problem by permanently assigning a factory-trained technician to each copier sold. This promise of long-term solutions for potential problems was a winner, which the company sales staff used successfully to take the office manager's focus off of price and quality, and redirect it to support.

Personal Attention

In this dehumanizing world of cookie-cutter products and services, there's nothing like special personal attention. Sears' Allstate Insurance built a business on it.

> *You're In Good Hands With*
> *Allstate*

● *Sherman Howe: Selling Help in a High-Tech World*

Sometimes the biggest opportunity for a reseller is helping a prospect overcome fear of the unknown, especially if it's in a new and complex category, like personal computers were back in the early '80s. The experience of the PC retail chain Sherman Howe

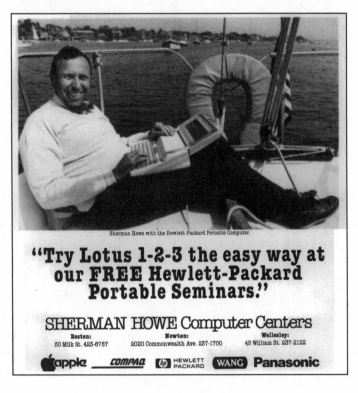

Sherman Howe with the Hewlett-Packard Portable Computer.

"Try Lotus 1-2-3 the easy way at our FREE Hewlett-Packard Portable Seminars."

SHERMAN HOWE Computer Centers

Boston:
50 Milk St. 423-6787

Newton:
2020 Commonwealth Ave. 237-1700

Wellesley:
45 William St. 237-2122

apple   COMPAQ   HEWLETT PACKARD   WANG   Panasonic

Computer Centers, founded by Sherman Uchill (with his name changed to Howe to reinforce its positioning) is an excellent illustration of how smart selling and personal attention can be used to motivate customers to take action.

Sherman Howe was targeting business-to-business sales. The company's primary objective was to get businesspeople to make contact so that Sherman Howe reps could make sales presentations to their companies. They were having difficulty, however, generating significant lead activity from their Yellow Page advertising and telephone cold calling. Their mission was to find out how they could get more leads and get in front of more prospects. Here's what the research indicated.

Sherman Howe Computer Centers

Question: "Why would you buy from Sherman Howe instead of other companies in the same business?"

Buying Index

At Sherman Howe we'll show you *how*
to use the equipment...179 winner

Sherman Howe is a leader in small business computer
systems with a national reputation...................106

Sherman Howe can act as your purchasing
agent...23 loser

Note: An index of 100 is an average response. A total of 300 interviews were conducted among prospects in the greater Boston metro area during 1981.

This research among potential business and professional customers revealed that the big opportunity was to personalize the Sherman Howe image and invite prospects to attend free hands-on seminars and executive workshops. There, the well-trained Sherman Howe professional sales force would provid special personal attention and demonstrate *how* to use the new systems in real business applications.

The personal contact at the seminars generated dramatically improved sales conversions. Sherman Howe became a leader in New England computer sales within a short time of instituting the free seminar program, and the sales force had a field day racking up sales from the leads that were generated.

● *Direct Tire's Untraditional Loaner Cars*

A retail expert we heard at a recent seminar proclaimed, "In the '90s you'll keep your clients by kissing them on the lips so hard it hurts." Well, Barry Steinberg's Direct Tire & Auto Service emporium, which caters to the Mercedes/BMW/Saab crowd in Boston, goes almost this far. You can get your tires, mufflers, struts, brakes, and shock absorbers replaced anywhere, but where can you get the free use of a loaner car while the work is being done? Research we conducted for Direct Tire's owner, Barry Steinberg, surprised us with the incredible appeal of good service, particularly when it came in the form of loaner cars for customers.

Direct Tire & Auto Service

Question: "Why would you buy your tires or get auto maintenance at Direct Tire instead of the store where you purchased the last time?"

	Buying Index
Free loaner cars	196 winner
No appointment necessary	100
Free safety inspection	57 loser

Note: An index of 100 is an average response. A total of 300 interviews were conducted among customers and prospects in the greater Boston metro area during 1979.

As Steinberg put it, "I knew our customers appreciated the special personal attention of being able to use a loaner car. We started with a few used cars which we offered customers with a request that they put a little bit of gas in when they returned them. When the research demonstrated how appealing this service was versus all the other aspects of our service, we realized the opportunity to expand the fleet of loaners and forget about asking people to add gas." The loaner cars have been so effective that Direct Tire's fleet now consists of over twenty-five new loaner cars at several locations.

The company carries through with other visible symbols of personal service as well. *Inc.* magazine, in an article titled "The Real Cost of Customer Service" (Sept. 1990), described the operation this way:

> Steinberg uses service to distinguish his shop from other automotive shops. When you enter his waiting room the differences become more apparent. The waiting room is immaculate. The magazines on the rack are current, with titles ranging from *Sports Illustrated* and *GQ* to *Vogue*. The coffee is freshly brewed. There are windows in every wall, allowing you to watch Direct Tire's technicians as they work. As you look around, you notice that the salespeople are in uniform, wearing shirts and ties with a baseball-style jacket that carries the company logo. Even the way they address you is different. 'I've never heard so many yes ma'ams and no ma'ams in my life,' says one 40-year old customer who has been going to Direct Tire for years. There are few bargains at Direct Tire, but customers are more than willing to pay for value, service, and convenience, and he's (Steinberg) constantly looking for new ways to let them do just that.

It's no surprise that Direct Tire was the only small business in New England profiled in the book, *Up Against the Wal-Marts: How Your Business Can Prosper in the Shadow of the Retail Giants.*[11]

Despite the fact that Direct Tire's prices are consistently a shade higher than the competition and net margins are twice the industry average, the company enjoys over $9 million in annual sales. Within three years of the introduction and promotion of loaner cars, Steinberg's monthly service business tripled, and gross margins on service are an amazing 42 percent! Direct Tire's sales have continued to increase every year since its founding in 1974, despite flat sales for the industry as a whole.

ACCESS Is Key

The moral of the story is that you haven't caught the fish until it's in the creel. Use several access arguments when setting the hook. You must make sure that all your hard work doesn't go to waste. But, of course, when they are ready to buy from *you* on the spot, be quiet and take the order!

Chapter

Step 5: MONEY Time

Money talks, nobody walks.

Anonymous

Will They Accept Your Pricing?

Will prospects accept your pricing? This is the big question when prospects reach the Money step. The key to winning at this step is to understand what goes on inside their heads. Handling the Money step is like playing cards: the more you know about the other person's hand, the better your chances of winning.

> **Why They Don't Buy: Big Mistake #5**
>
> If you assume you know their *pricing expectations* but haven't asked, you're probably wrong. This could lead you to use the *wrong closing arguments* and blow the sale.

You need to do three things *before* you can present your Money step arguments.

1. Use the key question we provide to detect *buying signals* that confirm your prospects are at the Money step.
2. Determine your prospects' *price expectation range*.
3. Understand how your prospects perceive the *value* of a product or sevice.

Buying Signals

You've heard about "buying signals" before. A buying signal indicates that prospects are interested in buying and probably have no substantial objections so far. "How much does it cost?" is one of the strongest buying signals. Once you hear it, you can proceed immediately to your next task, which is to determine your prospects' price expectations. But if you don't get this type of signal about your pricing, you won't know if they are ready to discuss it.

To determine if prospects are ready to buy and ready to talk about money, ask this *buying signal question* that Lee DuBois told us was the key:

> In your opinion, do you feel this (product or service) will give you the (results and benefits) you want?

The choice of the Commander word *feel* is intentional in this question and works for every profile type, because you really want a "gut-feel" reaction from everyone at this point. If prospects say yes to DuBois' question, you can move on to determine their price expectations. If the answer is negative, you need to smoke out and deal with objections.

Price Expectation Range

Most prospects have a range of price expectations for both your category of product or service, and your particular brand. For example, if you're selling office supplies, prospects will have an expectation of what these types of products sell for. And, based on the reputation of your firm and the particular brands you sell, they'll have some expectation of your prices.

If your pricing is within their range of expectation, closing the sale should be relatively easy. If your pricing is substantially *higher or lower* than their *price expectation range*, you will have more difficulty in closing the sale. So you need to find out what their price expectations are in order to figure out how to pitch your actual pricing.

The easiest way to nail down your prospects' price expectation range is to ask these two questions in this order:

1. Do you have a timetable for purchasing in mind?
2. Do you have a budget range in mind?

The expected budget range will immediately tell you which arguments to use based on whether they think you are *overpriced* or *underpriced*.

The Value Equation

If prospects are ready to buy, they will weigh the appeal of your product against the investment needed to acquire it. Prospects will buy from you:

- ❯ *If* the value of what you have to offer is seen as higher than the investment required.
- ❯ *If* your product is as good or better than expected.
- ❯ *If* your product is better than the competition (if any).
- ❯ *If* they have made a decision in your favor at all the previous decision steps.

That's a lot of *ifs*.

A prospect's determination of value is a mental calculation where the appeal of your offerings (some tangible, some emotional) is weighed against the investment needed to acquire them. Simply put:

Value = Appeal versus Investment

Why Your Price Is Right

Your goal at the Money step is to present arguments that enhance the *value* of your selling proposition by justifying the *investment*. Well-chosen and effective arguments will get you through the often difficult Money step and win you the sale.

The four most persuasive money argument categories are:

1. What's free (if you're overpriced)
2. Why so inexpensive (if you're underpriced)
3. Return on investment
4. Lower cost than the real competition

What's Free?

If your pricing is higher than your prospects' expectations, you have a real challenge, but one that you can overcome with the right arguments. The best way to deal with this is to point out what they get for free. Advertising people say that *free* is the best advertising word in the English language, probably in any language. In salesmanship, *free* is an effective way of justifying your pricing when it turns out to be higher than what prospects expect.

What's *free* are all the competitive advantages you have over the competition. For instance if you offer free delivery and your competitors don't, it's a powerful way to justify higher prices. This

is especially true when you're in a business like Subtractive Technology, delivering photographic materials on a rush basis to ad agencies and graphic artists, for whom time is more important than money (see ad opposite).

What's free can be emotional peace of mind when your product represents less risk. For example, both Saab and Volvo charge price premiums on their automobiles. But customers are willing to pay the added price when these manufacturers assure them that they and their loved ones will be driving the most crash-resistant cars on the road. That added margin of personal safety is part of the *value* of these high-priced automobiles. *Free* can also be physical, quality issues that set your product apart from the competition. For example, the world is awash in good quality table AM/FM radios costing less than $100. Many offer tape and CD player features. These radios are, in effect, a commodity product. Yet the Bose SoundWave radio commands—and gets—a price of $350. Why? Superior sound achieved through a unique design.

Pan Am played its *free* card by providing something that its competitors did not: free helicopter service for premium-class passengers.

Fly One.

Get One Free.

***Complimentary Helicopter Service
From JFK When You Fly Pan Am First
Or Clipper Class To New York.***

In a highly competitive field like health care, even if you're priced competitively, a *free* benefit that encourages members to stay healthy can help differentiate your plan from the competition and build strong customer loyalty.

● *Get Healthy, Get Rewarded for It*
New Hampshire-based Healthsource is on the cutting edge of

health care, promoting good health through fitness backed by *free* rewards. The plan provides members with fitness prizes, cash incentives, or a combination of both for keeping fit through regular exercise programs.

According to Ann Rohrborn, Vice President of Marketing Communications,

> We've learned that providing incentives for staying healthy helps our members take an active role in their own good health. Our signature fitness program, WORKING WONDERS rewards members for keeping fit through a regular exercise program. As a result, they're more likely to enjoy good health and less likely to require medical help so it's a win-win situation.

Our research confirmed the appeal of this approach.

Healthsource Health Plan

Question: "What aspect of Healthsource makes you most interested in switching to the Healthsource plan?"

Buying Index

Healthsource will actually provide incentives (fitness
   prizes, cash, or both) for staying healthy..........179 winner

Healthsource is one of the fastest
   growing plans..107

Healthsource offers discounts on
   maintenance drugs...47 loser

Note: An index of 100 is an average response. A total of six focus groups were conducted among consumers in New Hampshire and Massachusetts during 1991.

Donna Lencki, CEO, observes, "Our people have listened carefully to what members want and then delivered it. Maybe that's why Healthsource has been ranked among the best health plans in the nation by major publications including *Newsweek, USA Today,* and *U.S. News & World Report.*"

Healthsource's innovative approach to health care must have caught the attention of CIGNA too, because they're now part of the CIGNA HealthCare family of companies. The combined organization delivers medical benefits to 12 million people and dental benefits to 13 million. Hopefully, Healthsource will be allowed to retain its name and unique plan configuration, which we believe represents a welcome future trend in health care.

Why So Inexpensive?

Having the lowest price or being the lowest bidder will generally help your selling, but it can be a double-edged sword. In fact, if your pricing is out of your prospects' price expectation range, it can kill the sale for you altogether. Why? Because it raises perceived risk about your product and/or about you as a vendor. Very low prices are often equated with inferior quality or poor performance. To illustrate, there's a wonderful Gahan Wilson cartoon showing three astronauts lying on their backs in a space capsule awaiting blastoff. Two of the astronauts look confident and happy; the third looks very worried. You can't figure out why he's worried until you carefully examine the many control panels in the capsule and suddenly discover that he's looking at a little plaque in the corner that reads, "This capsule was built by the lowest bidder."

● *Ernie Boch, "Because My Costs Are Less"*

What you don't want to do is lose the sale because you have pricing so low that your prospects perceive you and/or your product as risky. If you feel you may be priced lower than your prospects expect, you need to defend your pricing to eliminate the perceived risk.

We have found that one of the most effective ways of justifying a low price is on the basis of *low costs*. And we've never seen anybody do this better than Ernie Boch. Ernie Boch is pure salesman. Here's how Ernie, New England's and one of America's largest car dealers and distributors, does it in classic stand-up television commercials that have been working for him for over twenty-five years.

> ### Ernie Boch: 30-Second TV Mitsubishi Dealer Ad
>
> *(Ernie points at you:) "Hi, I'm Ernie Boch, and I can sell you a Mitsubishi for less because my costs are less.*
>
> *"That's only natural.*
>
> *"We have no mortgages, strict cost control, and we buy our cars for cash.*
>
> *"So we can sell for less because our costs are less.*
>
> *(Ernie waves:) "C'mon down!"*

And come on down they do, in droves. Ernie's message is compelling because he gives you the details on *why* his costs are low.

● Colombo Yogurt: Classy Yogurt at a Classy Price

Back when we were on the ad agency side we helped launch Colombo Yogurt, now a national brand, into New England, its first market. It was an excellent product going head-to-head with Dannon. The client was planning to underprice Dannon, even though their costs were the same. However, when we tested pricing strategies we realized that underpricing could be a big mistake. We discovered that women felt that if Colombo Yogurt underpriced Dannon it could mean that it was an inferior product. Based on the research, we recommended that Colombo abandon an underpricing strategy and put the money into marketing and the bottom line instead. They agreed, and they priced Colombo at price parity with Dannon.

The parity pricing generated extra advertising dollars, which paid off. Within six months Colombo was the number one selling yogurt in New England. Within a year it became the number three selling yogurt in New York City (which is actually worth a lot more than being tops in New England).

As a salesperson, pricing is probably not within your control.

However, you can often upgrade what you present by suggesting a higher-priced version as an alternative, or recommending add-ons that enhance the perceived value of your offering.

Return on Investment

One powerful way to justify the cost of your product is to present it as an investment that will pay for itself. A return on investment story can help frame your prospects' thinking about the value of your product or service, and gives you a chance to recap sales arguments that most appeal to them.

● *At Louis Nothing Wears Like the Classics*

Back in the late '70s, if you were selling suits that retailed for over $1,000, even though they were perhaps the finest suits in the world, you better have had a solid selling platform to convince customers that the suits were worth the money.

Louis Boston was one of our first retail clients back then and the research we did for them still holds up today. When we met Louis' owner, Murray Pearlstein, considered by many to be one of the most savvy retailers in the business, his question was straightforward, "Faced with double-digit inflation and a jittery economy how do I justify the price of my clothing given that I'm not willing to sacrifice quality for lower price?" We discussed some of the possible support propositions, which tended to focus on the expertise of Louis salespeople, the wide selection of highest-quality clothing, and the European styling.

It was only after the research came back that we understood what it would take to justify Louis' extremely high quality and subsequent prices: a long wear, stay-in-style story which Geoff Currier, the Creative Director on the account, coined into "Nothing Wears Like the Classics." This was supported with classic styles and classic fabrics, which together paid off in greater functional usage, and a superior return on investment. The selling propositions scored as follows:

Louis Clothing

Question: "How do you justify the price of Louis clothing?"

	Buying Index
Good investment (updated classic style and materials last longer)......................186	winner
European styling. . .the forefront of men's fashion 110	
Sophisticated silhouette from our own forms...........38	loser

Note: An index of 100 is an average response. A total of 200 customers were interviewed in Boston during 1976.

As Arthur Jordan, one of Louis' most successful salespeople recently observed, "Even today when we're offering $3,000 suits from Brioni and Kiton in Naples, our customers appreciate that because we're using lighter, softer fabrics they can be worn for a longer season and won't go out of style. But they still appreciate that these suits are hand tailored by craftsmen with a history of making garments, not by a laser cutter."

Louis is still reminded by its customers that they appreciate how a suit they purchased there ten years ago continues to hold its form and remains fashion-appropriate. Geoff Currier, adds, "Today the word classic is overused, but it doesn't have to mean dull and boring. Now it's more updated classics with a little flair. Louis is really much more traditional than people give them credit for."

Today, Louis has found its niche and serves its customers so well that the retail expert Allan Flusser, author of *Style and the Man*, recently referred to Louis as the "best men's fashion store in the country, if not the world!"[12] And Stanley Marcus, Founder of Neiman Marcus, says, "Murray Pearlstein *is* the clothing business."

● *Selling an Underwater Survey System*

In the early '90s a leading international company making underwater survey systems was anxious to increase sales of its equipment designed to map the ocean floor using specialized techniques. Many countries bordering the world's oceans were in the process of buying equipment to map the ocean floor, but the company's sales force had not achieved the success they were looking for. This was particularly surprising to their engineers, who claimed that their mapping device, selling for $1.75 million, was the best product on the market, with deep mapping capability up to depths of 1,600 meters.

To get to the heart of the problem, we interviewed 100 key decision makers worldwide to find out why they weren't buying our client's system. While a few mentioned government resistance to foreign equipment and export policies, cost was cited as the key reason. In fact, 88 percent claimed they could not or would not spend over $1 million dollars on mapping equipment—no matter how good it was. Furthermore, 85 percent were not interested in mapping deeper than 700 meters!

How could this situation be remedied? Designing a lower-cost companion system capable of mapping to only 700 meters was a long-term possibility, but selling the current system on a *return on investment* basis turned out to be the winning alternative.

Ocean Floor Mapping System

Question: "What would motivate you to buy this $1.75 million mapping system over others on the market?"

Buying Index

It costs less to operate because it maps faster. It maps
accurately at speeds up to 20 knots ....149 winner

It's been accepted by the standards of all major
international governments 97

It costs more than other systems, but it maps down
to 1,600 meters depth while competitive
systems map only down to 700 meters ....26 loser

Note: An index of 100 is an average response. A total of 100 interviews were conducted worldwide among potential customers.

The cost of undersea mapping, we soon learned, is not just the cost of the mapping system but the total day-by-day costs of keeping the boat, the crew, and the mapping equipment working. Our client was able to demonstrate that their mapping system could do its work at twenty knots, compared to substantially lower speeds for competing systems. Given the total cost of ocean mapping, they were able to show that their higher-priced system would pay for itself in a surprisingly short time, after which point it would continue to provide a better return on investment than anything else on the water.

Lower Cost than the Real Competition

Whether prospects think your pricing is higher or lower than the competition depends on who is perceived as the competition. Løwenbrau ran an ad with a succinct headline that revealed its real competition.

> *If they run out of Løwenbrau...*
> *order champagne.*

Traditional ways of evaluating cost efficiency may make your product or service look like a loser, and those traditional ways may be deeply ingrained in the buyers you face every day. But if you think about it carefully, the typical ways of looking at cost efficiency may be inappropriate for your particular brand. What you need to do is reframe the debate and show that you are, if fact, lower in cost than the real competition. Cost efficiencies are usually represented as ratios, like the cost per thousand something-or-others. Since the costs on your price list are most likely a given, the secret is to redefine the real value basis of your product or service: the "something-or-others." Here's how Softrock did it.

● *Softrock Radio: The Eagles Without the Turkeys*
WEEI-FM, the CBS-owned FM radio station in Boston, was a pioneer in developing a radio music format that successfully featured a special blend of selections from the biggest contemporary

albums by artists like the Eagles, Elton John, Chicago, Joni Mitchell, and Carly Simon. The music format had previously been loosely defined as "The Mellow Sound" until CBS and Clark Smidt, the master music programmer at the station, carefully reworked the music blend and renamed it "Softrock," a name our research proved was a winner.

The Eagles.
Without the turkeys.

SOFTROCK
WEEI-FM 103

Maybe that's why we're #1 in reaching college grads.
Call 267-7000, ask for Jerry Charm, and we'll tell you more.

As soon as the new Softrock format was introduced, it attracted a more sophisticated, yet mass-appeal type of listener. Initially it did not attract huge numbers, but delivered sizzle and upscale appeal. Unfortunately, ad agencies traditionally compare radio station efficiencies on a "cost-per-thousand listeners" in a given age and gender range; by this measure, WEEI-FM Softrock didn't look like the great media buy it really was. The problem for the sales force was how to present Softrock pricing on a basis that showed it was a lower cost and a better deal than the real competition.

We suspected that the Softrock format was attracting a more affluent listener who had more money to spend on the finer things in life: fine restaurants, vacations and air travel, BMWs and Saabs, computer equipment, and other things that radio advertisers often push. In other words, the WEEI-FM format was attracting the "The Eagles without the Turkeys." Audience research for WEEI-FM showed that Softrock radio listeners spent about *twice* as much money on these luxury items than did the average radio listener.

The numbers looked like this:

WEEI-FM Radio

Question: "How often do you make the following purchases or participate in the following activities?"

Fine restaurant dining 328

Air travel..276

Foreign luxury cars..263

Computer equipment 245

Vacations..231

Note: An index of 100 is average. These indexes for WEEI-FM are 2 to 3 times higher than the average for all area radio stations. The research was conducted in 1978 among 400 consumers residing in the metro Boston area.

The station's sales presentation showed convincingly that while Softrock's cost-per-thousand listeners to advertisers was as much as 50 percent higher than competitive radio stations, the *real competition* was for the money listeners spent on the products being advertised. On this basis, Softrock was very efficient compared to other stations in the market! As one of the station's salespeople observed, "We made more money for CBS with Softrock than they had ever made with previous FM music formats. This 'class act' had long-lasting, high-performance sales power!"

Selling Your Money Arguments

The secret to presenting your pricing favorably is to know where you stand before you reveal your pricing. If you know what your prospects' price expectations are in advance, you can use the appropriate sales arguments to convince them that your pricing is both acceptable and advantageous as an investment.

Chapter

14

Follow the Path to Success

*If you keep doin' what you've always done,
you keep gettin' what you always got.*

FOLK SAYING

"It's too complicated. I can't remember it all."
"I tried it once or twice and it didn't seem to work."
"I feel clumsy selling this way. I think I'm much better
    selling the way I've always done it."
"I just can't seem to get the hang of it."

CHANGE NEVER COMES EASY. It takes extra effort. You make mistakes. You don't feel as strong or as confident as you used to. You don't feel like your old self. You forget where you are and sometimes even draw a blank. It's real easy to go back and do it the way you've always done it. But we don't think you're that kind of person. If you got this far, you have the motivation to dramatically increase your success through Buying Path Selling.

Seven Steps to Success

The question is, what's the easiest, most natural way to learn how to find a prospect's buying path and follow it to a successful sales conclusion? The answer is to start where you are, with what you know. As you work on what is most familiar to you and begin to create success, you can move on to the parts of the program that are less familiar to you. Here are the seven steps to success in using Buying Path Selling techniques.

1. Clearly Identify Your Dominant Buying Profile

Review chapter 3 to refresh your memory of the language and other clues people exhibit when they are in their dominant buying profile. Most people almost immediately identify with one particular dominant buying profile. To check out your own dominant buying profile, consider how another salesperson using buying profile techniques would identify you on first contact. While few people exhibit *all* the clues in a given buying profile, you'll most likely feel that you exhibit many of them, at least enough for another well-trained salesperson to identify your dominant profile.

Review chapter 7, and then chapters 8, 9, or 10, whichever presents the sales arguments most persuasive for your personal dominant buying profile. The power of the various sales arguments for your buying profile may not be in the same rank order for you as they are for others in your profile, but most of these arguments will be more convincing for you than for people in either of the other two profiles.

Review in your own mind a variety of buying situations in which you have responded very positively to salespeople. What language helped build your trust and confidence? What sales arguments did you find particularly persuasive? Did these salespeople sense where you were on your buying path? What similarities did you share with these individuals in how you view the world around you? Did they appear to be your *type* of person?

As you review your own reaction to other salespeople, you'll begin to get a much better feel for how prospects make buying decisions when they are in the same dominant buying profile as your own. When you feel comfortable with the variety of aspects of your own buying profile, you are ready to take the next step.

2. Identify Prospects in Your Dominant Buying Profile. Talk with Them in the Language of that Profile.

Prospects who share your dominant buying profile are generally the easiest to identify. In a sense, you already know who these people are. They are basically like you in terms of how they make sense of the world, how they talk, and how they make buying decisions.

Once you have identified a prospect as being in your dominant buying profile, try sharpening up your language skills to take maximum advantage of the persuasive power of mirroring that language profile. Your natural language will tend to favor words that fit your dominant profile, but it will also include key words from the other profiles as well. That's because the natural language of most people is a mixture of word types.

Review the list of key words and phrases for your dominant buying profile in chapter 3. Start using these consistently with prospects in the same profile. When you do, you'll build trust and confidence more quickly and more deeply. When you become adept at this, you will be ready for the next step.

3. Concentrate on Using Sales Arguments that Are Most Persuasive in Your Profile for Prospects in that Buying Profile.

Again review chapters 8, 9, or 10 to fix firmly in your mind the sales arguments that are most effective in your own dominant buying profile. This should be easy, because many of them are the ones you've personally responded to in the past, and probably used most often in past selling, regardless of who you were talking to. But there may also be a few arguments that you have not used very often in the past. Try using all that are appropriate for your product or service, concentrating on the right words and phrases for this profile. You'll find that your persuasiveness will increase with these prospects, even though you have typically been fairly successful with them before. Once you've sharpened your presentation to prospects in your own dominant profile, the next step is to do the same for all those other prospects.

4. Identify Prospects in Your Nondominant Buying Profiles. Talk to Them in the Language of Those Profiles

For many salespeople, this is the hardest step. Because the specific language, words, and phrases we use naturally are so ingrained, so unconsciously formed, that they are virtually automatic. Your natural language profile is like walking, almost like breathing. But once you've mastered this step, the rest is easy.

Start by answering this question: After your own profile, what's the next easiest profile for you to identify and mirror? Which set of mirroring words and phrases are easiest for you to use in place of what you naturally use now? To find out, review the remaining two profiles and their word lists in chapter 3 and then pick the word list that you find to be the easier of the remaining two. Practice on these first. Again, if you need more clues to help you decide which is easier for you, try mirroring the language of prospects who are in the easiest of your nondominant profiles. You will start to see immediate results. Even a few key words and phrases that mirror your prospects' profiles will gain positive responses that you have rarely been able to generate before from these people. You're on their wavelength and they know it! The enthusiasm generated by this experience will easily carry you through the rest of the program.

When you are confident that you can handle the language profile of the easier of your two nondominant profiles, the obvious next step is to master the third and final profile. By now you've become adept at using one "non-native" language profile, so mastering the third profile will be easier than the previous step. You are also now well on the way to developing a dramatically more powerful and comprehensive set of sales techniques.

5. Sell to Prospects in Your Nondominant Profiles Using the Most Powerful Sales Arguments for Each Profile

This is actually easier than mirroring your nondominant languages. You can prepare the arguments in advance, and have the materials ready at hand to use when you need them. Be sure to practice your presentation so that you can consistently use language and sales arguments that match each other during the initial parts of a sales presentation.

Multiprofile selling in a one-on-one situation is discussed in chapter 11. This refinement can be very effective, but it's not easy to achieve fluency. Don't worry about selling a Commander sales argument with Thinker language until you feel very comfortable selling your sales arguments with their matching languages. If you have initially established trust and confidence with language and sales arguments that match your prospects' dominant buying profile, answering objections and additional questions in the language you have already prepared will work well enough as you gain experience with these techniques.

6. Perfect Your Expertise in the DREAM Buying Path Steps

Knowing where your prospects are the DREAM buying path—and selling accordingly—is a critical part of selling. Many revert to evaluation sales arguments even if the prospects aren't at the Evaluation step. The typical result is a lost sale. Review the DREAM buying path often, and make sure you are addressing the real buying needs of your prospects by giving them what they need to move along the path to a sale.

7. Take This Book to Your Sales Manager

If your sales manager didn't give you this book, give it to him. The sales manager can do something very quickly that you probably cannot do on your own: obtain the survey research that you need to nail down the most powerful arguments for the products and services you sell. Few companies ever do the homework or survey research that reveal the truly *knockout* arguments. Instead, they pack their sales kits with arguments that someone *thinks* or has a *hunch* will get customers' attention and interest. Or they depend on you to ferret them out through lots of time- and prospect-wasting trial and error.

If the examples cited in the preceding chapters tell you anything, it's that most *hunches* aren't nearly as powerful as those identified through research. We've done it over and over again for big and small companies in every category of product and service sales. The results are vastly better than anecdotal evidence or what trial and error can provide.

Wrapping It Up

The most important message in all of this is that people are different. The way they talk, the way they think, the way they make decisions, and where they are in the decision process is always different. And, the odds are that they are different from you. But once you know how to hear how they talk, spot where they are on the buying path, and discover how they make decisions, you can Talk the Talk, Walk the Walk, and Tell the Tale in ways that will dramatically increase your sales effectiveness. Finally, you can avoid the five big mistakes that lead to lost sales.

Using any part of Buying Path Selling will increase your sales effectiveness, your self-confidence, and the fun and joy of selling and persuading. The more of it you use, the better it gets. You can use it with prospects, customers, your boss, your subordinates, and with your colleagues. You can even use it with your spouse. Anyone you use it with will appreciate it, because it shows that you understand where they are coming from, and that you have the respect, intelligence, and common sense to respond to how *they* deal with the world around them.

Notes

1. Richard Bandler and John Grinder. *Frogs Into Princes*. Moab, UT: Real People Press, 1979.

2. Ted Levitt. *The Marketing Imagination*. New York: The Free Press, 1983.

3. Brian Tracy. *Advanced Selling Strategies*. New York: Simon & Schuster, 1995.

4. Lee Dubois. *The Lee Dubois Course in Selling Techniques*. Boston: The Lee Dubois Co., 1976.

5. While specific parameters might be established for a given project, the underlying methodology is consistent, and all the results have been established as quantitatively rigorous. In each case, a number of respondents were asked to rate several propositions with regard to a question or statement, and the results were tabulated using a weighted scoring technique. All data was then indexed so that the average response would be measured at 100, and all responses weighted against the average. Any response indexed at over 100 indicates a higher level of preference, and any response indexed below 100 indicates a lower level of preference. Throughout the book we have presented the results of such studies, by highlighting the three responses that represent the highest score, the lowest score, and an average score.

6. Translation from Burton L. Mack. *The Lost Gospel*. New York: HarperCollins, 1993. Parentheses modified from the original.

7. Marvin Minsky. *The Society of Mind*. New York: Simon & Schuster, 1985.

8. Daniel Dennett. *Consciousness Explained*. Boston: Little, Brown & Company, 1991.

9. Stephen Pinker. *How the Mind Works*. New York: Norton, 1983.

10. Howard Gardner. *Frames of Mind*. New York: Basic Books, 1983.

11. Don Taylor. *Up Against the Wal-Marts: How Your Business Can Prosper in the Shadow of the Retail Giants*. New York: American Management Association, 1994.

12. Allen Flusser. *Style and the Man*. New York: HarperCollins, 1996.

Index

Permissions Acknowledgments

Chapter 1, page 1: Willie Nelson quote reprinted with permission from Mark Rothbaum.

Chapter 3, page 22: Photo of General MacArthur courtesy of Corbis.

Chapter 3, page 29: Photo of Albert Einstein courtesy of Corbis.

Chapter 3, page 34: Photo of Walt Disney, © Disney Enterprises, Inc.

Chapter 12, page 157: Excerpted from Yogi Berra's *The Yogi Book*, Copyright © 1998 L.T.D. Enterprises, used by permission of Workman Publishing Co., Inc., New York, All Rights Reserved.

The authors gratefully acknowledge the permissions granted for reproduction of marketing and promotional materials from the following: Avery Dennison (chapter 5), Blue Cross/Blue Shield of Rhode Island (chapter 6), Cambridge SoundWorks (chapter 8), Eastpak (chapter 8), Fountainhead Technologies (chapter 10), Kryptonite Bike Locks (chapter 9), Lappen's Auto Parts (chapter 6), Louis Boston (chapter 13), MediSense (chapter 10), Monson Chemicals (chapter 10), Mount Snow Golf School (chapter 9), Odd Job (chapter 6), PŪR Water Filters (chapters 5 and 6), Sherman Howe (chapter 12), Subtractive Technology, Inc. (chapter 13), Tech HiFi, Unitarian Universalist Association (chapter 9), WEEI-FM (chapter 13).

About the Authors

Harry Washburn is Chairman of Wallace & Washburn Inc. A native New Yorker, he is a graduate of Dartmouth College and the Harvard Business School, where he studied under the legendary Ted Levitt. For many years he served as an account manager at the advertising firm of Benton & Bowles, where he introduced a number of successful products, including Orange Plus, Fortified Oak Flakes, and Glade Sun Country. He teaches courses on marketing management, new product development, and advertising management at the Harvard University Extension School. He lives in Cambridge, Massachusetts.

P. Kimball "Kim" Wallace is President of Wallace and Washburn Inc. After growing up in Seattle, and graduating from the University of Massachusetts in Amherst, he joined Exxon, where he became the leading salesman in New England. He has worked as an account manager at the advertising firms of Doyle Dane Bernbach, and Norman Craig & Kummel, and at SSC&B, where he pioneered the research that led to repositioning of Noxema moisturizing cream. He lives in Wellesley, Massachusetts.

Wallace & Washburn

The authors met in Boston when both were named VPs and Account Supervisors at Humphrey Browning MacDougall, then the largest advertising agency in New England. They formed Wallace & Washburn Inc., based in Wellesley, Massachusetts, in 1976 as a marketing company specializing in sales and marketing research and consulting. Since its inception, Wallace & Washburn has been in the forefront of innovative sales marketing research techniques, developing ThoughtScan, the Argument Audit, and most importantly, the Decision Path Analysis techniques that are the basis of this book. They have also founded American Sales Training And Research (A-STAR), to provide sales consulting and customized training materials for corporations and sales training firms—using the DREAM path approach and W & W sales research.